FOLK SONG of THE AMERICAN NEGRO

JOHN WESLEY WORK, A.M.
Professor of Latin and History
Fisk University

NEGRO UNIVERSITIES PRESS
NEW YORK

The Library of Congress cataloged this book as follows:

Work, John Wesley, 1871–1925.
　　Folk song of the American Negro.　New York, Negro Universities Press [1969]
　　　131 p. illus., music, ports. 23 cm.
　　　Reprint of the 1915 ed.

　　1. Negro songs—History and criticism.　　I. Title.

ML3556.W78　1969	784.7′56	73-98736
SBN 8371-2790-4		MARC
Library of Congress	70 [4]	MN

Copyrighted, 1915
F. A. McKENZIE
Nashville, Tenn.

Originally published in 1915 by Fiske University Press, Nashville, Tennessee

Reprinted in 1969 by Greenwood Press, Inc., 51 Riverside Avenue, Westport, Conn. 06880

Library of Congress catalog card number 73-98736
ISBN 0-8371-2790-4

Printed in the United States of America

10 9 8 7 6 5 4 3

Dedication

To

"dulce decus meum," "animae dimidium meae,"

Agnes.

JUBILEE HALL (FROZEN MUSIC).
Erected by the Original Jubilee Singers. It stands on the site of an old slave pen.

CONTENTS.

	PAGE
Introduction	5

Chapter I.
| African Song | 7 |

Chapter II.
| Transmigration and Transition of Song | 16 |

Chapter III.
| American Folk Song | 26 |

Chapter IV.
| Characters and Peculiarities | 35 |

Chapter V.
Number and Classification	44
Joy Songs	45–49
Sorrow Songs	50–54
Sorrow Songs with Note of Joy	55–60
Songs of Faith	60–62
Songs of Hope	62–64
Songs of Love	64, 65
Songs of Determination	66, 67
Songs of Adoration	68, 69
Songs of Patience	69, 70
Songs of Courage	71
Songs of Humility	72

Chapter VI.
| Birth and Growth of Certain Songs, with Exposition | 76 |

Chapter VII.
| Agencies of Preservation and Development | 90 |

Chapter VIII.
| The Tour of the Original Jubilee Singers | 101 |

Chapter IX.
| What the Negro's Music Means to Him | 110 |

Chapter X.
| A Painted Picture of a Soul | 122 |

ILLUSTRATIONS.

	PAGE
Jubilee Hall	2
"Daddy Comin' Home"	13
Mrs. Sheppard	79
Mrs. Moore	81
Original Jubilee Singers	102
You May Bury Me	115

MUSIC.

	PAGE
I Couldn't Hear Nobody Pray	24
Somebody's Buried in the Graveyard	34
Balm in Gilead	43
This is a Sin-Trying World	75
Steal away to Jesus	89
Were You There?	100
I'm Going to Do All I Can	109
Swing Low	121
Lord, I Want to Be a Christian	131

INTRODUCTION.

WHEN Fisk University was chartered after the close of the war the treasurer was moved to devote his leisure hours to the instruction of the pupils in vocal music. Their voices and progress were both a surprise and delight. Five years later the Jublilee Singers of the University sang before the National Council at Oberlin. Leading Congregational ministers and laymen from all parts of the land were thrilled not only by the sweetness of their voices and the accuracy of execution, but were charmed also by the wonderful feeling of the plantation melodies which were entirely new to them. As a member of that Council in 1871, I was present and well remember the marvelous magic of their song with its accompanying rythm and the revelation it gave of the Negroes' religious nature and experience. This was the introduction to the American people of the folk songs with which the Jubilee Singers of this University went on a triumphant tour around the world, the new world and the old.

It is a far cry from that day of the introduction of these folk songs which has their expression and birth among the days of bondage, and which have been faithfully preserved and steadfastly cherished for the light they give in their quaintness of expression upon the experiences which call them forth, and for the exquisite melodies which touch a chord that the most consummate art fails to reach.

Professor Work not only presents a remarkable collection of these folk songs of his race, but in the study of their evolution and history he brings an interpretative and enlightening analysis of their characteristics and qualities with a literary expression which is only second to the songs themselves, and which will richly repay attention. As one of a race whose historic life in this country is so recent, Professor Work understands and realizes how it is that the accumulated strength of a patient overcoming of trials on the part of souls in their aspiration and struggles, called forth the inspiration of these songs, while God in the hard processes of His providence was leading His people to a permanent inheritance. For many years an honored professor in his Alma Mater, like the original instructor of the Jubilee Singers, Professor Work has turned from his classes in Latin to assist in his leisure hours in the musical education of students, especially to keep in mind the days in which these folk songs sprang into light. All added attraction to this choice collection of melodies of the people of his race are those of his own composition, which have already won their way into the pleased recognition of all who have heard them.

A. F. BEARD,
Secretary American Missionary Association.

FOREWORD.

BECAUSE most of the material for this book required the investigation of original sources, it has required more than a decade to bring the work to completion. So much of what has been written on the subject of the "Folk Song of the American Negro" has been positively inaccurate and unreliable, that I deemed it proper to learn the story from the songs themselves and from the makers of the songs.

This has sometimes meant hunting in out-of-the-way places, attendance upon church services here, there, and yonder, in season and out of season. It has meant in some cases, years of search for some special information, sometimes following the trail from state to state. Sincere efforts have been made to verify the statements and propositions herein, and though some of these statements seem almost incredible, I beg the reader to understand that very much of the history and description has come to me first hand from those who have been a part of them. No supporting authorities have been adduced save those that are considered wholly reliable.

The work was undertaken for the love of our fathers' songs. It has brought me much real pleasure and now it is sent forth in love. My cordial gratitude is herewith expressed to Professor Adam K. Spence, who taught me the value of these songs; to Mrs. Ella Sheppard Moore, who taught me so much about them (these two of blessed memory); to Miss Mary E. Spence, for many valuable suggestions, and to scores of others who have been patient with me, answered so many, many questions and have given me the information which has made this book possible; to Miss Jennie A. Robinson, who has so largely directed my musical inclinations and inspired my musical efforts; and to Miss Dora A. Scribner, who so kindly criticized my manuscript.

JOHN WESLEY WORK.

Nashville, Tenn., April, 1915.

CHAPTER I.

AFRICAN SONG.

"*Wo man singt, da lass dich ruhig nieder
Böse menschen haben keine lieder.*'

THIRTY centuries ago, amidst the dawning civilization of the Mediterranean shores, science taught that the earth was a circular disc surrounded by the ocean. Contemporaneous legends told of the swarthy Ethiopians living in two divisions; one in the extreme East, the land of the rising sun, and the other in the extreme West, the land of the setting sun. Consequently the Ethiopians dwelt in perpetual light.

This light was symbolic of their own souls; pure, bright, and happy. So worthy were they that the Gods from Olympus honored them with regular visits. Homer in narrating these events calls them the "blameless Ethiopians," and Vergil speaks of the black Memnono, the King of the Ethiopians, as the son of Aurora, the Goddess of the Morning and of Light.

Ruthless centuries have not overcast that brightness, nor have they destroyed the soul happiness of the Son of Light. His soul is a song. He expresses his every experience, his whole life, in terms of melody and he passes through the Valley of the Shadow of Death with a song upon his lips. Studied through his music, the African, living in cruel savagery and black heathenism, becomes less a savage, less a heathen, for he sings a song intensely human which strangely touches human hearts. This savage, this heathen, sings of the harvest, of love, of life, of death, and of the god whom he elects to serve.

The songs of the tribes differ as tribal life differs. This difference however, is not important, for in the essentials all the songs are wonderfully the same. Mountains, rivers, forests, valleys, lakes, plains, —in fact, all natural surroundings and manifestations,—make their distinct impressions upon the tribes and in some marked respects render them different. But in the deep life forces there is oneness. This difference and this oneness are both clearly portrayed in the music of the African.

All tribes have constructed their music upon the verse and chorus plan. There is a verse sung by a leader, and the chorus follows. The leader is generally chosen for his voice and his superior knowledge of the songs. This peculiarity has remained fixed as the song of the African has come through the receding centuries. There are some songs in which the African heathen shows his kinship to other heathen, namely, in the almost uncanny chants generally wailed as accompaniments to the war dance. This chant still lives a life of strength and freshness in the Negro's musical world, bidding fair to reach a greener old age and finally to evolve into some form of music, rare in charm and beauty. In America we hear it and see it acted in the barn dance, on the stage, in the streets among the children; in fact, many an occasion is enlivened by this species of music, the interest in which is intensified by the rhythmical patting of hands and feet. This rhythm is most strikingly and accurately brought out in their work songs. For some reason or other, the African seems to work his best to a musical accompaniment, sung, whistled, or hummed. Especially is this true when the laborers are numerous and in "gangs". The men sing and their music seems irresistible; for their bodies sway, and their hammers rise and fall to the perfect time of their tune and the work goes on with happiness, interest, and power.

The most plausible reason for the African's working to tune seems to be, that above all modes of expression this swarthy man loves the musical mode, and his almost riotous emotions are forever clamoring for expression. This makes his life a life of song. And the song has upon him a somewhat intoxicating effect which gives strength and spirit to his being. This strength and this spirit thoroughly possess him, both soul and body, making his body tireless and his soul happy.

Among the Kroo tribes it is a custom to change farms frequently, because their god forbids their cultivating the same farm during successive years. Consequently every year new lands must be opened up, necessitating the felling of trees. Three or four surround a tree to cut it down. Gala leads a song but does no cutting. This Gala is the leader of all songs and shouts. In war time he stands in the midst of his warriors, hurls his spear into the air, catches it again and leads a shout, which is a vigorous kind of song, telling of the valor of their ancestors, and describing what they themselves are going to do in war, such as bring back the head of the conquered king on a stick. This same Gala in times of peace and in times of land-clearing leads a song, which, translated, runs thus:

> Youthful tree!
> We must cut all around it
> Gala's tree!
> We must cut all around it
> Cawlaw, Cawlaw, Cawlaw, Cawlaw.
> We must cut all around it.

Gala sings what might be termed the verse, setting the tempo for the strokes of the axes and in soft melodious chorus all the choppers join, imitating as best they can the sound of the axes striking the tree, "Cawlaw, Cawlaw, Cawlaw, Cawlaw."

It is most likely that when this song is sung, four men are doing the cutting, since this number striking one after the other fits in exactly with the rhythm of the song. There must be other songs, however, to accommodate different numbers of choppers. The Kroo, from whom this information was gained, stated that three or four men surrounded a tree and cut it down.

Whether it be of war or of peace, the song the African sings is a gem of the melody of motion, full of human spirit, sometimes mild, sometimes wild, oftentimes bright with sublime flashes of poetry; at all times weird.

War Song.

> O that Great Bird of War!
> Thou hast made this town silent.
> They come, they come
> Creeping down low
> Among the tall grasses,
> The enemy come.

The meaning of this song is clear. One tribe has destroyed the village of another and this apostrophetic lamentation bursts forth from the souls of the conquered.

Before going to war the Kroomen assemble to drink the palm wine five days old. It is an intoxicant and acts doubtless as all such drinks, exaggerating one's idea of his own powers. The Kroos consider this intoxication a gift of physical power and courage from their god, preparatory to the mighty struggle awaiting them. Gala takes his place in their midst, hurls his spear skyward, catches it, and they all sing:

"We are about to drink of the palm wine."

Then the leader, Gala, sings:

"I have not drunk of the palm wine,
So you need not put me out of the town,
Truly you are my soldiers."

This song in its completeness must most assuredly have leaped out of spontaneity. While the soldiers all drink freely of the palm wine, the general, Gala, is not allowed to drink at all, for though the soldiers are supposed to be in a blind fury, the leader must have full possession of his mental faculties so as to lead his army aright. If he drink the wine, he is banished from the town.

Death casts the same darkening shadow over the heathen African that it casts over more enlightened souls. To him, as to others, it is the same soul-trying, heart-breaking mystery, and before it this black child of heathenism stands in awe, helplessness and final resig-..ation. When a soul's "took its flight and gone home" into the far off somewhere, and those to whom it was dear have gathered around and taken the "feeble body and carried it to the grave," the pain is just as poignant, the experience is just as overwhelming to them, as to the rest of God's children.

Whatever his feeling may be, he expresses in his own weird way just as much as any of us could possibly say; for no multiplication of words can express finer, stronger, or sweeter sentiment than that which he expresses over the clay of him whose soul has gone with the "Pale Horse and his Rider."

"Eonlay zeer marco	"Fare thee well,
Eonlay yonga songa	Fare thee well,
Monga eonlay zeer	On thy far-off journey,
Marco way marco	We shall carry thee to the hill."
Marco way marco	
Mama."	

The African folk song is naturally quite free from the tender expressions of love which we know and understand so well, for just as she is among all other heathen peoples, so is woman among the Africans,—an inferior being to serve and fear man, her superior, her lord. She performs much of the drudgery and practically makes the living for the family. While her husband sits comfortably in the shade smoking his pipe and perhaps telling stories to a companion, the wife with her baby strapped upon her back, sows, tends, and reaps the casada and rice. On the other hand, man is a being of might and power whose every wish, however, trifling, must be a law unto her; while he is a law unto himself. She is slave, he is master; and the relations commonly existing between master and slave are cruelly maintained between them. Under such conditions there is no deep love and where love does not abide there can be born no such tender expression of the "divine passion" as is found among Christian people. It is Christianity that has taught the true loveliness of woman and the true nobility of man. Those love songs that make our hearts throb in harmony with every note and syllable of their divine sentiment are expressions of those hearts alone that believe woman to be an angel and man just a "little lower than the angels." Such an intelligent recognition of the divine within us; such homage to that divinity; such tender yet powerful affection for the beautiful in woman and the noble in man,—these all have their sources and nature in souls that have been touched and enlightened by a God of Love.

The heathen's god is a god of frowns and of vengeance; of storm and of destruction; of might and of power; some Zeus who "shakes Olympus with a nod." The African sings his love in these words:

> "My lover is in yonder town,
> So I also must hurry to be there,
> For, oh! my lover shall be my husband."

The American Negro sings:

> "Sun lights up all de big blue skies,
>   Shines all de live-long day:
> Silvah moon and de star's bright eyes
>   Drives all de darkness away.
> But what is dat to de light dat gleams
>   In dis merry heart of mine ?
> I luv her true an' my luv jis beams,
>   Beats all de sun dat shine.

"Mockin' bird, oh! he sings so fine,
  Wa'bles his surenade;
Lark, he sing in de bright sunshine;
  Catbird sing in de shade.
But whut is dat to de pretty song
  Dat rings in my heart all day?
My luv is true as my life is long,
  An' it's goin' to stay dat way.

"Rose, it bloom, oh! it bloom so sweet,
  Fills all de summer air;
Vi'let blue underneaf my feet,
  Sen's sweetness ev'rywhere.
But whut is dat to de flowers dat bloom
  In my heart as on I go,
An' fills all my life wid sweet perfume?
  Beats all de flowers I know.

"Light may shine, it may shine so bright,
  Flowers perfume de air;
Birds may sing all de day an' night,
  Sen' music everywhere;
But de brightest light an' de sweetest flower
  An' de prettiest song I know
Jis' fills my heaht every live-long hour,
  Jis' case l luv her so."

The love song with its lack of color and spirit is in bold contrast to the lullaby with its interesting features. True to nature, the crude children of the Overshadowed Continent "gather their goods where they find them" and sing of the things they know best. While her American sister sings:

"Daddy's comin' home, my dahlin', hear him a-whistlin' low;
Leave po' daddy jis' one kiss, honey, 'fo' you go;
Den close dem eyes, my honey, deah, dem brown eyes tenduh bright,
For God an' angels, mammy's luv, will watch till mawnin' light;
Den sleep, my honey, baby dahlin', sleep—"

the African mother sings:

"Nar ju pentee,
  Nar de an mo ne clay
Key geelo ply
  An moo moo Ken po—"

"My child, lie down,
Your mother's gone to the farm
So the Great Spirit will bear
You on his back."

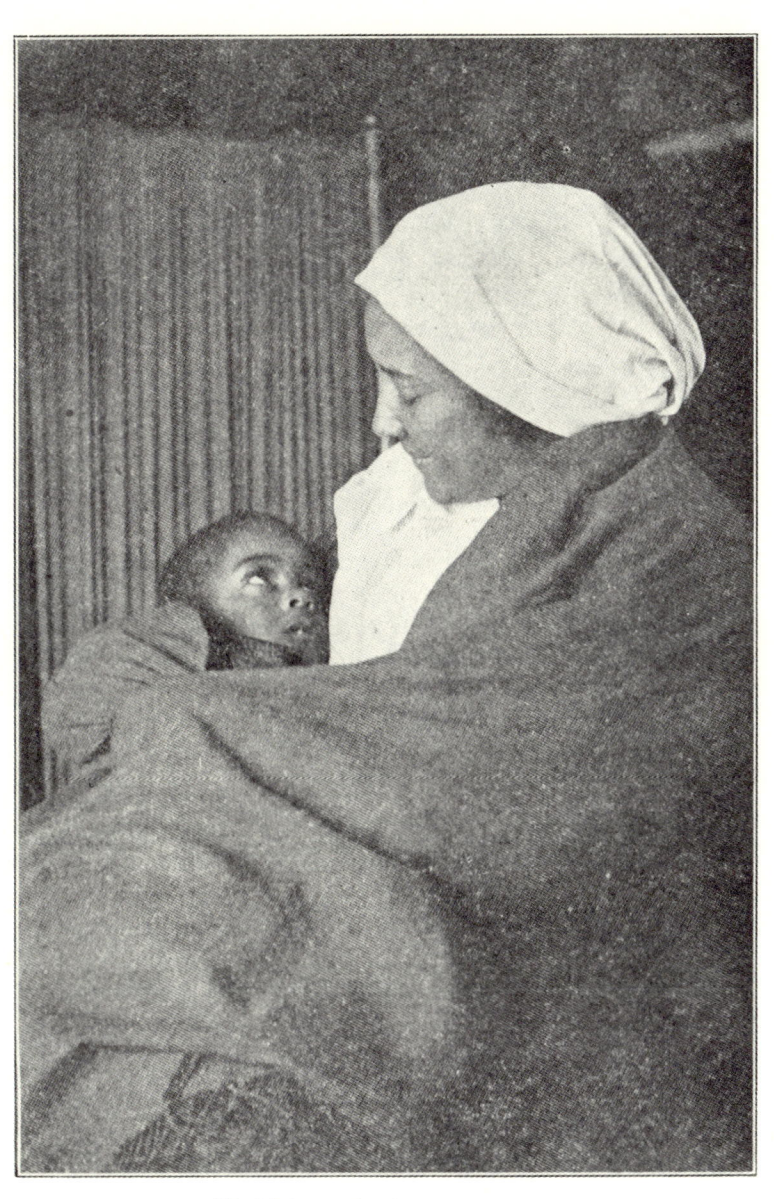

"Daddy's comin' home, my baby,
  Heah him a-whistlin' low;
Leave po' daddy jis one kiss,
  Honey, fo' you go."

To grasp the meanings of *Folk Songs* is oftentimes difficult because of the workings of the crude minds whence they sprung, as well as because of the passage of the songs from locality to locality and from generation to generation. Different surroundings, different dialects, different occasions or times of inspiration, all tend to work changes in these songs. Consequently there is often more than one explanation for the same song. This little lullaby may correctly be explained in the following ways:

(1) The tired mother, at even tide, is trying to inveigle her baby into sleep; the baby, however, accustomed to sleep in the sling upon the mother's back while she works in the fields, shows some unwillingness to go to slumberland, and finally to overcome that objection the mother promises that the Great Spirit will bear baby upon his back.

(2) It may be that at this particular time the mother had some reason for leaving baby at home and so promises baby a cradle in her absence upon the back of the Great Spirit.

(3) It is possible that this lullaby did not have its birth in the heart of a mother, but in the anxious spontaneity of an elder brother or sister or even a father (while the mother was absent), for caring for baby in mother's absence gives rise to many a song, many a means of amusement, many a soothing dose.

When baby is troublesome in his journey to bye-low-land, the mother has recourse to another "sleep song," and just as our mothers frightened us with "rag-man," "peg-leg," "boogoo-man," and "rawhead and bloody-bones," the African mother calls upon the witch.

"Kan, Kan, O some bay, O,
An noo you Kan."

"Witch, O great Witch,
You will take all bad children."

This witch song is sung in high, throaty tones in an effort to frighten the child as much as possible, and it is easy to believe that the wild shriek of the voice would arouse in baby's mind a wish for any other land rather than the land of wakefulness.

Though it is generally agreed that through music the soul is fully and most truthfully expressed, still there are evidences pointing to the fact that there are closer relations between the soul and musical expressions than have been satisfactorily explained. These relations can be felt, but any accurate description seems beyond the grasp of man's mind.

Why do certain races use certain scales while others use different ones? It is quite clear why certain peoples have certain subjects for their songs; why some sing of mighty oceans, storms and waves, and some others sing of blue skies and olive groves, but why one race from the very beginning of its existence will express its sentiments in tones different from those of any other people is a mystery yet unsolved.

The African soul for some inexplicable reason expresses himself in its own peculiar scale, 1-2-3-5-6-8. Every shout of triumph, every note of endurance, every wail of sorrow, every cry of pain, every heart-throb of love, every prompting of religion, is expressed in that scale, and moreover, expressed in such wise, that as a result the quality of wierdness is the essence of each one. Let the African sing of victory, and although the notes stir men's hearts to deeds of heroism, those same heroic hearts will express themselves through genuine tearfulness; let him sing of defeat, and the strangeness of it all with subtle force takes from defeat the sharpness of its sting; let him sing of the toils of an every-day, humdrum life, and the very tools with which he labors, the drill, the hammer, the ax, play such a queer and fascinating tune that others are led to believe that the African's existence is an undisturbed succession of bright, cloudless days; let him sing of Heaven, and a weird rapture so completely possesses the soul, that this beautiful world of ours, the grand firmament above us, are just commonplace, and a desire for the celestial world displaces all other longings.

In truth, the African Folk Song is a melodious expression of tribal life with an irresistible weirdness running through the whole.

"It is a soul breathed into Melody,
A heart living in a song."

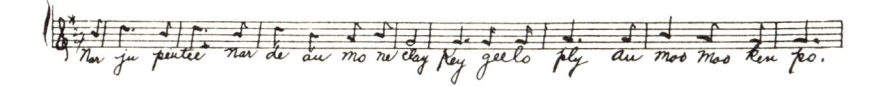

CHAPTER II.

Transmigration and Transition of Song.

"What bird is that? It's song is good."

IN the year of our Lord, one thousand six hundred and nineteen, the same year that marks the birth of popular government on this western continent and only a short time before the Puritans, who had sacrificed home for conscience sake, landed at Plymouth Rock, there sailed up the James River a Dutch man-of-war. This vessel came to port at Jamestown, and there, in return for provisions, bartered to the settlers, twenty human beings, dark children of darker Africa. From what port or tribe they came is not known; the name of the ship as well as that of the ship's master, are also unknown. In fact, the only reliable information concerning the whole transaction is found in the chronicles of John Rolfe, the husband of Pocahontas, which make mention of a "Dutch man-of-war who sold us twenty Negars." It is probable that these twenty "Negars" were snatched from some point on the west coast of Africa. That such an event, so full of mighty possibilities, should be so veiled in uncertainty, is itself a deep mystery and leads us straight into these lines of Cowper's:

> "God moves in a mysterious way
> His wonders to perform."

The voyage had been long and wearisome; and to those children of the tropics, bound and fettered, it was like passing through the fires of purgatory. Then, too, everything was so new and overwhelming that their souls were plunged into abysmal despair. Many a time they had faced the spears of their enemies; many a time they had tasted the bitterness of defeat; they had struggled for life with the wild beasts of the forests; but now life had changed, and everything was so new, so strange; home was so far away in another world, that all its dearest relations had vanished into fading dreams, which, nevertheless, started bitter pangs of longings and sorrows that would not die. The past was dead, and freedom was no more. Henceforth they must serve other men whose thoughts, languages, and lives; whose very God were all strange and unknown. The whole panorama was so stupendous that these simple-minded children were cruelly crushed beneath its awfulness. Welcome the spears of the enemy; welcome the savage wild beasts of the forests! They groped through the darkness toward the faintest gleam of light. To us, the sons of these pitiable heathen, who have seen greater miracles than the parting of the Red Sea, the falling manna, the feeding of the five thousand, and the raising of the dead; to us who have seen the wrath of men praise Him, it is all plain. They wept and sowed in the darkness; we rejoice and reap in the light. Many of His ways are past finding out, but with the question, "Shall not the Judge of all the earth do right?" we leave it all with Him, for—

> "Deep in unfathomable mines,
> Of never-failing skill,
> He treasures up his bright designs,
> And works his sovereign will."

Those broken-hearted strangers soon accepted the situation they could not change, and unlike the ancient Hebrews who hung their harps upon the willows and sat weeping by the rivers of Babylon, they, through their bitter tears sang a sweet song, a weird song, a new song in a strange land.

Why these men who had just cause for rebellion against a fate so cruel and whose struggle for freedom would have been applauded by all who believed in right and justice; why these men who through centuries of living with nature and amidst perils had grown mighty of limb and of courage, chose to sing and not to curse, from a human standpoint is akin to miracle. It is one of those psychic phenomena which show the inscrutable workings of the Creator. Whatever the force that led them to bless and curse not, one thing we do know; the New World heard his song, listened, wept, and rejoiced as the strange musician play a sympathetic accompaniment upon the heartstrings of human kind. When the Trojans fled from their burning city to make a new home in Italy, they left all save their household gods. When the Hebrews went into captivity they could not sing, but they wept when they remembered Zion. They carried Jehovah their God into a strange land. When the Africans were snatched away to the new world to fell the forest and cultivate the fields, they left their all save their song. This they brought, because the All-wise knew the *New World* had great need of it. The New World was henceforth to be their home and they could speak the language, live the life, and worship the God of the New World, but in their own peculiar melody they would express their new world experiences. From that time their song began a subtle and gradual change from African to American.

The evolution of African to American song correctly indicates the corresponding evolution in the African himself. The process was thorough, and both singer and song became American. In proportion as the life of the New World was above that of Africa, in proportion as the light of this New World was brighter than the dim haziness of the dark continent, in that same proportion is this new song brighter and more spiritual. Loftier things are treated with a more blazing religious fervor.

The religion of the Negro has long been a subject of much diverse criticism. It has even been mocked and jeered. Church services have been sources of mirthful entertainment. Philosophers and learned men have pointed to the Negro's religious outbursts, his shoutings and rejoicings as marks of ignorance, superstition and heathenism. Most assuredly these are not the most approved methods of worship, nor do they measure up to the ideals of the highly cultured, but they at least have an explanation which might lead to a better understanding, and sometimes a better understanding leads to a higher respect.

Whatever else the Creator has given to other children, He has given to the African a heart as responsive to the forces of life as an eolian harp to the evening's zephyrs. His pains are poignant, his joys are ecstatic. He is either on the mountain top or deep down in the valley. The plains make no strong appeal to him. This heart of the African is of a distinctly religious nature, expressing itself in building houses of worship, and in the fullest enjoyment of devotion. The fact that worship is man's duty does not always appeal to him. Indeed, the joy and happiness of it have almost effaced the idea of duty. He worships not so much because he ought, as because he loves to worship.

Moreover, the religion of the God we worship makes its strongest appeal to the burden bearers of the world. "Come unto me all ye that labor and are heavy laden and I will give you rest," has always been a most effective invitation to the black man. For who could possibly be more weary than he, who could possibly be more heavy laden, who could possibly enjoy rest more than he? To him this has always been a real invitation to a truly heavy-laden man. His religion has always been a real power that relieves real burdens. Christianity to him, has been more than religion, it has always been from the very first, an experience. The Spirit beareth witness with his spirit.

True it is that this "shouting" is sometimes overdone; sometimes it is spurious. Nevertheless it is most often a genuine expression of souls that are glad, glad in the living reality of a religion whose God lightens burdens and wipes sorrow's tear away; glad in the living assurance of an eternal life without burdens and without tears. It is natural and quite to be expected that the Negro should shout. His emotional nature has been so deeply wrought into for generations by bitter pangs of sorrow, that when he contemplates the promises of the Christian religion, he is wholly overcome and he expresses his ecstacy in "Glory! Hallelujah!"

With his transition from African heathenism to American slavery, the Negro set up an altar dedicated to the God of love. Blessed phenomenon, under such circumstances to give up his gods and all his past for this new God. What wisdom! Slavery never begets love. The very thought of being owned is abominable. It is naturally a source of antipathy and animosity, hatred, revenge. It even sometimes leads men to question the justice of the God who permits it. The human heart cannot perceive righteousness in being torn from those it loves, from the memories and attachments that make up the happiness of life, to be forced to labor hard and long that another may eat, rest, and be comfortable—yea, to suffer and die at the whim of a master. This is surely beyond a mortal's comprehension of justice. Still through all these crushing experiences, the Negro slave trusted God. What faith! The transcendent thought that there existed somewhere a trustworthy being who has promised never to forsake him, but to turn his sorrow into joy, has ever been enough to make him shout. This shouting has been and still is his means of expressing adoration; it has been also for all his pent-up emotion, a safety valve. Blessed be Providence that taught him to shout. This "shouting" is in no wise essential to religion, though it is often an evidence of it. Measured by the standard of Christanty, how does the "shouting" Negro stand? Look around and see. What good has he wrought? Has he not abounded in good works? Who laid the foundation of our religious and educational life? Who gave and still is giving to support all the uplifting agencies of our life? Who has lived more strictly up to the standard of love and sacrifice? Who founded our Christian homes? Whose faith has ever been stronger; whose prayers more effective? Whose courage greater? Whose labor more productive? Whose religion has had severer tests? Whose religion has come forth from these tests more triumphantly? Answers to these questions will draw one up face to face with the conclusion that our untutored Negro mothers and fathers who praised and are still praising God in loud "Glories" and hallelujahs did praise and still praise Him also in spirit and in truth.

All phases of his regeneration are expressed in his new song, and that is why the world loves to hear him sing. He sings life. His song is new in thought and spirit. It chants new life. The vehicle, save one small, weird part, is as old as the African himself. This vehicle, the framework of his musical creation, has remained ever the same, and even the new life, though powerful, has not been able to change it. Africa fashioned the body, but America breathed into it the breath of Life.

No influence has been able to change the predominant feature of the melody. The employment of certain notes to form his scale, the arrangements of these notes to gain certain idiomatic effects, the general mould, consisting of verse and chorus, with variations and its perfect rhythm, all of which suggest the term "form" remain essentially the same. The American Negro, however, has wrought some development into this form. He has, because of an intelligence superior to that of his African brother, evolved some more beautiful tunes by more effective arrangements of the notes of his scale. He has added strength to the melody and, in some degree, has polished and refined some of the barbaric tendencies. The most striking development has been the use of syncopation to which the American Negro has given such charm that a contagion of syncopation has spread and taken strong hold upon the music of today. Any further development in this direction would seem impossible; certainly, if it could be done, it would be insufferable. But its present use is the great contribution of America to Negro melody.

Music expressed in the "form" described in the foregoing words, is as natural to the American Negro as his breath. No other form could satisfy his soul. Indeed, it is a portrayal of his soul, and is as characteristic as are his physical features. Hear him sing in his church, hear him preach, moan, and give "gravery" in his sermon, hear the washerwoman singing over her tub, hear the laborer singing his accompaniment to his toil, hear the child babbling an extemporaneous tune, and most or all, these features will be recognized. Even those Negroes who have been educated and who have been influenced by long study, find it difficult to express their musical selves in any other way.

In addition to a development and a certain perceptible refinement in some phases, the American Negro has made a new kind of song out of a combination of two different kinds of African songs. That monotonous chant with the ever-recurring interjections, a prominent characteristic of heathen music, was evidently too tiresome and unattractive to him. It did not at all express the emotions born of his new world experiences. His vision was broadened now, and this chant, expressive of his heathen life, was too limited for him, so the first combination resulted in the following character of song. It has the qualities, both of the chant with its interjections and of the song with verse and chorus.

> "This is a sin-tryin' world—Oh, Lord!
> This is a sin-tryin' world—Help me, Jesus!
> This is a sin-tryin' world—In trouble!
> Oh, Heaven is so high, and I am so low,
> I don't know if I'll ever get to Heaven or no."

The first three lines with their different interjections, expressing the feelings of the leader, correspond with the original chant of the heathen Africa, and the two final lines are additions made by the American Negro. He went further and made another combination by adding a chorus to the chant and interjection, an example of which is one of the most interesting, beautiful, and pathetic of all our folk songs:

> "Couldn't hear nobody pray—."

Another curious as well as interesting addition made by the American Negro is a real groan which he introduces. There were times when the very depths of pain and sorrow were sounded, the awfulness of which was beyond his power to speak, but the pent-up feelings must find some expression which would as nearly as possible, represent in essence the pain itself. The spontaneity of his nature brought forth the little linguistic anomaly "um." How well it serves its purpose! How completely does it give expression to that emotion for which words are too weak! In the revival services when sinners were called to the "mourners' bench" to mourn and mourn and mourn in their struggles to "get religion," the Christians agonized to help them "come through." They prayed, sang, and wept. Under such conditions, the following song was born:

"Po' mourner's got a home at last—"

Under the power of this song, many a sinner has been convicted of wickedness and converted to a new life. Strangely enough, this linguistic anomaly was used to express not only depths of sorrow but also the heights of joy. There were times in the Negro's life when his joy and hope were beyond all words or too good and sweet to be spoken, and this was the only way in which he could express himself. The expectation of rest from unrequited toil gave birth to this song:

"Um—Most done toilin' here—"

There is one more notable difference in the song of the American Negro which is a sublime improvement upon the song of his ancestors. It may be an omission, intentional or unintentional. It certainly is a subtraction or an elmination. Whatever it is, it has the quality of the divine. In all his song there is neither trace nor hint of hatred or revenge. It is most assuredly divine in human nature, that such a stupendous burden as human bondage, with all its inherent sorrows and heart breakings could fail to arouse in the heart of the slave sentiments of hatred and revenge against his master.

Doubtless the essence of the Negro character epitomized and concentrated in the character of one man, furnished the lofty inspiration that gave birth to the expression, "No man can drag me so low as to make me hate him." Doubtless it was for such a time as this that he "came to the kingdom." Doubtless he was chosen by God to enounce this sentiment. Such a development of race character shows plainly divine intention. The world needs to know that love is stronger than hatred.

With the changing of conditions and experiences, with the passing of the years, the African became an American, and the melodies of Africa were evolved into American song, and this song is the Song of Love.

> "He whom love rules, where'er his path may be,
> Walks safe and sacred."

I COULD'NT HEAR NOBODY PRAY

*The interjections used here are not the only ones which can be used, but may be changed according to the emotions of the leader.

† Let this stanza be exceedingly slow, about half as fast as the others, and the chorus very soft. But go into the refrain a tempo.

I COULDN'T HEAR NOBODY PRAY—Concluded.

On my knees! couldn't hear nobody pray, A-
In the Jordan!
Troubles over!

With my burden! couldn't hear nobody pray, A-
Crossing over!
In the kingdom!

And my Saviour! couldn't hear nobody pray, O Lord! A-couldn't hear nobody pray.
Into Canaan! O Lord!
With my Jesus! O Lord!

CHAPTER III.

AMERICAN FOLK SONG.

*"I sang, and singing, forgot the wrongs
Of blind fortune and cunning foes."*

CIVILIZATION wears away the spirit and conditions which give birth to Folk Song. Bearing this in mind, it is not difficult to understand why there is no folk song which expresses the soul of America. America was settled by people who came from countries whose civilization was centuries old and who brought their institutions, customs, literature, and music with them. They were stronger than their surroundings. They had developed strength building nations which they had now abandoned. This strength was successfully used in fashioning and moulding their new surroundings after their own ideals. Their work was to build a new nation, by felling the forests, tilling fields, building roads, cities, harbors, and making laws. They came, the Englishman, the Scotchman, the Frenchman, the Scandinavian, the German, and the Spaniard. Common interests with wondrous power welded them into one. But the beginnings were too far advanced, the surroundings too conventional for folk song creation. Each brought his own song from his fatherland. So, strictly speaking, there is in the comprehensive acceptation of the thought, no American Folk Song. There is, however, a real indisputable folk song in America—an American production. It was born in the hearts of slaves and consequently expresses the life, not of the whole, but of a part, of our country.

From the very moment of his arrival, all conditions were favorable to the Negro's producing a folk song. Heaven and nature worked in harmony with the soul of the simple heathen to generate the spiritual atmosphere: the man-directed forces of the new world furnished the stimulus, and the emotional and musical soul of the simple heathen accomplished the rest. The African was vastly different from the other men who came to America. He was not fresh from a civilization which had lived through centuries, he had not been the builder of a mighty nation, he had not the means of conquering this rugged land, he was not stronger but weaker than his surroundings in America. He did not appropriate, but was appropriated; he did not assimilate but was assimilated; more than any other immigrant he became American, and to-day he is the American of Americans. Had conditions been different, it is certain that the trend of his folk music would have been in another direction. It was slavery that gave color to his music. Slavery was the starting point and Heaven was the goal of his life. The sorrows of slavery pierced his heart and it poured itself out in such lamentations as:

(1) "Nobody knows the trouble I see—"
(2) "I'm troubled in mind—"
(3) "O wretched man that I am—"
(4) "Before I'd be a slave—"

Songs of this kind express the tragedies of slavery. They are the depths of his music. Curiously enough, the slave held Satan accountable for all his troubles. His mind could reach no lower. At the other end, the upper limits, we find God and Heaven. To him Heaven was a place of relief from the ills of slavery and a land of eternal joys. The thought of Heaven winged his soul to flights of imagination that wafted it into a state of consuming ecstacy. Then he sang of "golden slippers," "starry crown," "long white robe," "golden harp," and all the adornments that made Heaven so real to him. Or he raised the question, "What kind of shoes?"

Who could tell the meaning of golden slippers to him who had worn brogans or no shoes at all? What did a long white robe mean to him who had known no better raiment than sacks, bags, or at best the roughest and poorest of clothing? What would it mean to him to have a starry crown, the adornment of a king, upon that old beaten and despised head of his? To him, those golden slippers and long white robe were as real as his brogans and his tattered garments.

His soul was either with Satan in pain or with God in joy. He hardly had time to see and appreciate the things of an every-day life. His surroundings were almost always extraordinary. This fact accounts for both the uncommon character of his religious songs, and the paucity and utter worthlessness of his secular songs. So few and so inferior are these latter that we may justly state that the Negro Folk Music is wholly religious. True it is that there were corn huskings, camp meetings, barn dances, and so forth, but it must be remembered that the corn husking was work as serious as plowing and hoeing; that the camp meeting was religious and in those days the barn dance was almost a priceless luxury. These periods of relaxation were so rare that they could not make any such impressions upon the Negro's soul as did those experiences that made up almost his whole life. Stephen Foster's old melodies, "Sewanee River," "Kentucky Home," "Nellie was a Lady," "Massa's in the Cold, Cold Ground," and "Ole Black Joe," are sometimes called plantation melodies. They were composed by a white man, and, therefore, cannot be placed in the catalog of Negro Folk Songs; still it can correctly be stated that in spirit and pathos they bear the Negro stamp, and it is not improbable that they are composed of stories and airs Mr. Foster learned from the Negroes he knew so well and among whom he lived during the days of slavery. Consequently it is not out of place to state here the paradox that these are the finest secular Negro Folk Songs in existence. There have been many imitations of Negro music and some of it has been enjoyable, but these songs of Stephen Foster stand out as the best of that class, in fact they stand alone, in a class between all other imitations and the genuine Negro Folk Song.

When the question of American Folk Song was first raised in this country, and some bold man ventured the opinion that the only American folk music was that produced by the Negro, immediately there was vigorous protest, but such eminent authorities as Dvorak and Kiehbiel, after careful investigation, have come to the same conclusion. As soon as this proof positive was given to the world, there arose another question. Is this music original with the Negro? The implied answer was "No." Now, as soon as the world recognized the worth and importance of this music, the Negro was called upon to prove himself the producer. It was contended that he got it from the Scotch, from the Portuguese, from the Indian, or more vaguely, from the European.

Dr. Richard Wallaschek in his book on Primitive Music, makes this statement: "I may say that, generally speaking, these Negro songs are very much overrated, and that as a rule, they are imitations of European compositions which the Negroes have picked up and served up again with slight variations." "Overrated?" In what way? In that they are called original or in the claims to the possession of value? "Imitations of European compositions which the

Negro has picked up and served up again, with slight variations"? What compositions? What variations? Let us look into this. "Overrated." If overrated in the point of originality, it is in the claim that they bear no trace of any other influence outside the character of the American Negro. Of course, this is not a fact, for the songs of the Negro can be unmistakably and plainly traced to African tribal songs. In scale, intervallic relations, rhythm, construction of melody, picturesqueness; in short, in vehicle, in frame work, there is very little difference between African tribal songs and the songs of the American Negro. To be sure, America has added something, and in some places pressed a stamp, but the dominant features are African. Again "Overrated!" If in the claim to the possession of real value, then Dr. Wallaschek certainly cannot have made any adequate study of these songs. "Value!" Why, the value of such songs as "Swing Low, Sweet Chariot," "Steal Away to Jesus," "Lord, I Want to be Like Jesus," can no more be overrated than the beauty of the distant "Jung Frau," or that of a moonlight night of southern June. In the presence of either, the soul is helpless to express itself.

"Imitations!" It would be folly to attempt to deny the fact that the American Negro's music shows some resemblance to the music of other peoples. This is natural, since all races have certain points of resemblance. But to assert that he has found any greater resemblance between the Negro's music and European music than would naturally result from the oneness of human nature, lays the writer open to the suspicion that he is uninformed, misinformed, superficial, unscientific, or all of these.

A study will reveal the fact that the Negro music is more unmistakably stamped with the Negro's character than is the music of any other people stamped with the character of the race which produced it. The characteristics and peculiarities of this music are discussed in another chapter. "Variations!" To this there is one very good explanation. It may be that Dr. Wallaschek has heard the Negro sing the "long meters" of Dr. Watt and other hymn writers. If so, he certainly heard such variations as never man heard before! For the Negro is able to take one of these hymns and sing it in such voice that it will seem more than an "European composition, picked up and served up again with slight variations," for he can run up and down the scale, make side trips and go off on furloughs, all in time and in such perfectly dazzling ways as to bewilder the uninitiated. In truth, the uninitiated would not recognize the best known hymn sung thus, unless he could catch a familiar word every now and then. Another example of variation may be found in such songs as "I've Been Redeemed." The chorus is Negro, but the stanzas of "There is a Fountain Filled with Blood" are used. Every feature of this song proves that it was composed in large degree and is not really a folk song, although it is classed as one. The burdens of bondage made the one overwhelming impression upon the Negro and kept him faithful to God, the Burden-Bearer; and to Heaven, where burdens are no more; these, therefore, are the subjects of the Negro Song.

It cannot be controverted, that in certain qualities the Negro's music resembles the music of other people, but that is natural, in fact, just as natural as that the Negro himself has certain qualities common to all men. There are points of resemblance and similarity in all the music that has ever been produced by any people, however different in race, or however far separated by ages. In essentials, all men have been and are still the same. The oldest form of African song, that monotonous chant with frequent interjections, strikingly resembles the music of the Indian. This is the form of all heathen music. It is an evidence of the oneness of the human race. The resemblance, however, between the music of the Indian and that of the Negro ceases at this point. In other respects, the difference is amazing. The nature of this very difference is, in itself, a conclusive argument that the Negro did not get his music from the Indian. It is just as reasonable to contend that a full blood Negro could be born of full-blood Indian parents. There is no strength in the argument that the Negro has developed the Indian's music into what we call Negro Folk Song; for it is impossible that this development could have been carried on to the point where not one trace of the original remains. In scale, intervallic changes, spirit, melody, rhythm, there is no trace of the Indian in the Negro's music. It is all Negro. On this point, Mr. Damrosch says: "The Negro's music isn't ours, it is the Negro's. It has become a popular form of musical expression and is interesting, but it is not ours. Nothing more characteristic of a race exists, but it is characteristic of the Negro, not the American race. Through it a primitive people poured out its emotions with wonderful expressiveness. It no more expresses our emotions than the Indian music does." On the other hand, however, it is passing strange that with the same skies above them, the same earth beneath them, the same mountains, valleys, and streams round about them, with the same environs touching them at so many points, the Negro and the Indian produced music different in every respect save that in which the music of all primitive peoples resembles.

The strongest resemblance between the Negro's music and that of the Scotchman is at the point of melody. Melody with flow is common to both, but the Scotch melody is the more developed. The Scotch music, also, sometimes strikes that wild note we find so commonly in the Negro music; in one or two instances the "Scotch Snap" has been found in the Southern Melodies, but it is not at all clear why these facts should prove that the Negro got his music from the Scot. Evidence that in essentials and peculiarities there is marked difference, in truth that there is no resemblance, seems irrefutable. Then even a casual examination will show the impossibility of the very thought of Scotch origin of Negro song. The Scot sang of war and vengeance. A man of blood, he sang of the sword. He sang the song that the Negro could not sing, for the Negro had faith in Him who said, "Vengeance is mine." When the black man sang of the sword, it was of the "Sword of the Spirit." Furthermore, the Scot's song is lacking in the element of sacredness which we find pervading all the Negro's music. For psychological and ethnological reasons, it is not strange that there are great differences.

How the African could have received his music from the Portuguese is beyond reason. It is true that Portugal is near one point of Africa, but how was this transmission accomplished? Did the Portuguese go among the Africans transplanting their music, or did the African come to Portugal and imbibe Portuguese melody? Suppose, however, there were such intercourse and opportunity for such transmission. Is it believable that the Portuguese song was so strong and so pervasive that it supplanted whatever music the African possessed, or gave to all African music characteristics the Portuguese music itself does not possess? The strongest evidence against a Portuguese source of African music is that the likenesses are so few and so slight and the differences are so many and so marked. Furthermore, when, where, or how did the Indian, the Scot, the Portuguese come into such powerful contact with the Negro as to teach him a song which accurately expresses the Negro's soul and the Negro's soul alone? When we see a flower with all the characteristics of the rose, and with those of no other flower, we never trace its source to the sunflower, but to the rose seed. When we see a magnificent tree, with growth, body, spreading boughs and leaves of an oak we never trace its source to the elm seed, but to the acorn. So the conclusion is irresistible that the music which expresses the characteristic of the Negro's soul alone, was produced by the Negro alone. It would be a miracle if such a soul as his did not produce a music all its own. "Of all the undeveloped races, the Negro seems to be the most gifted musically," says one notable musical authority. His emotional soul possessed of melody expresses itself in those unmistakable terms which portray the Negro as nothing else can.

Dr. Henry E. Kiehbiel, in an article upon the subject of Negro Spirituals, written for the New York *Tribune* September 12, 1909, makes the following statement: "Very slowly the study of folk song in its musical and literary aspects is acquiring scientific value as a sub-division of Folk Lore which in turn is a branch of the science of Ethnology. To this study America's most interesting contribution has been derived from the black people who tilled the fields of cotton and of rice in the days of slavery. This peculiar interest comes from two sources, the songs of the slaves are practically the only American products of their kind which meet the scientific definition of Folk Song; that is to say, they are the only songs of which we possess a significant number, which were created by an ingenious people, to be an expression of their feelings, as a whole. Nowhere, save on the plantation, could the emotional life which is essential to the creation of true Folk Song be developed. Nowhere else was the necessary meeting of the spiritual cause and the simple agent and vehicle."

More than a quarter century of study has given Dr. Kiehbiel, one of the very few men whose opinions can be profitably sought regarding Negro Folk Song, a deep and comprehensive knowledge of the subject, such a knowledge as to render him an authority. Facts bear out the statement of Dr. Kiehbiel that the songs of the slaves are practically the only American product of this kind which meet the scientific definition of Folk Song. These songs certainly express the feelings of the Negro "as a whole," and these "feelings" are just as certainly expressive of the life of the Southern States of America.

A people's musical expression of their feelings as produced by the forces and conditions of their life constitutes their folk song.

Carl Holliday, M.A., instructor in English Literature in the University of Virginia, says: "Of all the builders of the nation the Negro alone has created a species of lyric verse that all the world may recognize as a distinctly American production." Mr. Holliday has shown a warm interest and satisfying knowledge of the Negro Music. He approaches his subject with an adequate idea of its importance, treating it in a deservedly serious manner and producing an article, which is a distinct contribution to the subject.

The American History and Encyclopœdia of Music, under the heading "Negro Music and Negro Minstrelsy," contains the following statement: "While not of a strictly American origin, they have undoubtedly gone to form the foundation of such Folk Song literature as this country possesses." While this statement adds strength to the claim that the Negro has produced the only American Folk Song which is so far developed and improved in its vehicle that it is not far from the truth to call it American, the statement needs explanation. It is true that the Negro Folk Song is not wholly American, for the vehicle or framework is African. The literary and spiritual forces, however, are wholly American. The subject-matter and sentiment express American life. There is evidence of no other source. Recognizing both its Americanism and its worth, Dvorak in his "New World Symphony," Chadwick in his "Second Symphony," and Schoenfield in his "Sunny South Overture," Kœger in his "Ten American Sketches," have all used the essential materials of Negro music. Thematically, its use is becoming more and more extensive.

Musical and literary authority through scientific investigation has established the fact that while there is no American Folk Song in the sense of expressing American life as a whole, still there is a Folk Song in America, and that is the Music of the Negro.

*SOMEBODY'S BURIED IN THE GRAVEYARD

Somebody's bur-ied in the graveyard, Somebody's bur-ied in the sea,

Going to get up in the morning a shouting, Going to join Ju-bi-lee.

1. Al - though you see me com - ing a - long so,
2. I have some friends be - fore me......... gone,
3. Some - times I'm up, some - times I'm......... down,

To the prom - ised land I'm bound......... to go.
By the grace of God I'll fol - low on.
But still my soul is heaven - ly bound.

* Death held a very prominent place in the mind and songs of the slave. In exact proportion to his hardships, did he sing of death and the glories of Heaven where he should receive just those things that were here denied him. Heaven was to him above all else a place of *rest* and of shouting and jubilation.

CHAPTER IV.

CHARACTERISTICS AND PECULIARITIES.

> "The man that hath not music in himself,
> Nor is not moved with concord of sweet sounds,
> Is fit for treasons, stratagems and spoils;
> The motions of his spirit are dull as night,
> And his affections dark as Erebus;
> Let no such man be trusted."

IN spite of the continued contact with the whites, the Negro melodies as we have them to-day still retain their exotic traits."

It is the aim of this chapter to point out these exotic traits and other elements which give individuality to our Folk Song and as far as possible to give the reason or reasons for these characterizing and peculiarizing features. By far the most prominent and weighty influence in this music, as we have often reiterated, is its religious element. Each song is based upon some scriptural passage or it is created by the imagination out of a religious experience. This scriptural reference may not always be used accurately, in fact, it may be and often is twisted and changed in strange manner, but it is never wrought into a form so shapeless as to be unrecognizable; moreover, it is generally shaped so as to carry a *point which sticks.* Some of those based upon direct scriptural passages are:

> "Swing low, sweet chariot—
> Coming for to carry me home—"
> "I look over Jordan."—2 Kings 2: 1-11.
> "There is a balm in Gilead."—Jeremiah 8: 22.
> "Rise, shine, for thy light is a-coming."—Isaiah 60: 1.
> "I know I have another building."—2 Corinthians 5: 1.
> "Daniel saw the stone."—Daniel 2: 34.
> "Come down, angels."—John 5: 23.

Scores of songs come under this head in which the scriptural reference is most direct.

Among those songs which the imagination creates out of its religious experiences are found:

"Great camp meeting."
"Shout all over God's Heaven."
"What kind o' shoes you goin' to wear?"

Though these songs indicate a certain imagination they also show clearly that Heaven to the Negro slave was a real place with crowns of victory for all who bear the cross in the "low ground of sorrow." In marshaling biblical facts and history, some of these songs are astonishing, interesting, and in the display of ingenuity in fitting these facts to rhythm, are comparable to Homer's "Catalogue of the Ships."

(1) "We read in the Bible and we understand,
Methusaleh was the oldest man;
He lived nine hundred and sixty-nine,
He died and went to Heaven, Lord, in a-due time."

(2) "We read in the Bible and we understand,
Samson was the strongest man;
Samson went out at a-one time,
Killed about a thousand of the Philistine;
Delilah fooled Samson, this we know—
The Holy Bible tells us so.
She shaved off his hair, just as clean as your han',
His strength became as any other man."

(3) "Joshua was the son of Nun;
God was with him, till the work was done;
He opened the window and began to look out,
The ram's horn blew, an' the children did shout,
The children did shout, till the hour of seven;
The walls fell down, an' God heard it in Heaven."

"My soul is a witness—"

There are still other stanzas to this song, but these suffice to make clear the thought. Someone has stated that if the Bible should be lost, it could be recovered and reconstructed from the mind of the Negro. This seems to be and doubtless is an extravagant statement, but conversation with a Negro preacher, even of the uneducated class, will oftentimes cause wonder that such a one could be so full of an accurate knowledge of the Bible text. Some who can read just a little, and some who cannot read at all, can go on and on with citations and references, giving rapidly and off-hand, the book, chapter, and verse containing the scriptures which bear out what happens to be their views. They always have "views," and are always ready to defend them. In preaching a sermon they take their text, sometimes reading it from the Bible, sometimes reciting it, then close the Bible and proceed to the argument. This sermon, delivered without hesitation and without notes, is often a strange blending of imagery, poetry, and oratory, glowing with religious fire. The peroration of this sermon is intoned or "moaned." In other words, it is sung, and the effect upon the audience is visible. This moaning, singing or as the Negroes themselves call it, "giving gravey," is quite natural to the Negro. His proneness to sing shows itself in his every activity. Nothing is more to be expected than that when his activity is religious, in which above all activities he is most interested, he should throw away all restraint and conventionalities and be his natural self, which is a musical self.

This manner of preaching is not at all approved of by the later generation of Negroes; that is, the educated class, because it is a mark of the lack of intelligence. That is true, but it is a mark of naturalness. Education and civilization, along with the many good things they bring, bring also an unnaturalness.

The reason why the Negro songs are so full of scripture, quoted and implied, is that for centuries the Bible was the only book he was allowed to "study," and it consumed all his time and attention. This reason finds added strength in the Negro's religious nature.

Another characteristic of the Negro song is, as has been stated before, that it has no expression of hatred or revenge. If these songs taught no other truths save this, they would be invaluable. That a race which had suffered and toiled as the Negro had, could find no expression for bitterness and hatred, yes, could positively love, is strong evidence that it possesses a clear comprehension of the great force in life, and that it must have had experience in the fundamentals of Christianity. "One shriek of hate would jar all the hymns of heaven.

The rythm of this music is the element which has been most generally imitated and appropriated by the composers of to-day. Especially is this true of those who write popular music, both secular and sacred. This rhythm is a distinguishing feature of many of our most effective gospel hymns, and with heightened syncopation, another idiomatic peculiarity of Negro Folk Song, it gives "ragtime" its currency and popularity. "Ragtime" is an ingenious and fitting appellation for the music to which it gives a name, for it is time torn to tatters, but in such rhythmically fascinating manner as to arouse every single motor nerve of our being. That is why we like it, say what we may. The element of ragtime which makes it objectionable is the language and thought, not the vehicle, for were the vehicle objectionable we would discard some of the choicest music we now possess and cherish. Against the words and moral ideas of ragtime songs all respectable people, those who love aright, have just complaint; but let the spirit of ragtime be changed and let the writers of it express high ideals, instead of the low ones they now use, and the public, all, would welcome it, and hail it as a new development of the musical art. In the simple music of ragtime is a naturalness which appeals to nature. This rhythm in folk music, as hinted before, is idiomatic and is as essential to the body of our music as pure red blood is to the human body. A fresh, vigorous flow carries the life-giving forces to all parts of the system. In the Negro's character there is a quality which rhythm alone expresses. This quality is as striking and as characteristic as rhythm is in his music, and, furthermore, it is as evident in his life as rhythm is in his songs. When the Negro sings with the "Spirit and the understanding'" not only with his voice does he sing, but with his body as well. This body or corporeal accompaniment is contagious, and audiences often pat the feet, sway the body or move the head "in time." Some instances have been very noticeable and amusing. At a concert given by a company of Fisk singers in a Kentucky town, the audience was composed of students and teachers of a certain academy. The contagion of rhythm was so general that the concert was almost "broken up," because the singers could scarcely withstand the sight of almost the whole audience swaying in perfect time to their songs. Rhythm arouses emotion and emotion arouses motion. That is the explanation of the Negro's keeping time with his body while he sings. Imperfect rhythm he abhors quite as profoundly as nature abhors a vacuum and he has interesting and effective means of avoiding such a fault. Long holds are not natural to this music; and whenever they occur they indicate a development of the years subsequent to the days of Folk Song creation. The movement in this music, which largely contributes to what Dr. Krehbeil calls "Moving beauty," demands short notes and short syllables. To gain this effect, the creators of these songs have resorted ingeniously to the use of a nameless little something represented by the letter "A," thereby adding a subtle force to the song in which it is employed.

In that beautiful hymn "Lord, I Want to be a Christian," we find in the refrain instead of "In my heart,"—"In-a-my heart." In "Good News," we find, "I don't want-her leave-a-me behind." In "Judgment Day," we find, "Judg-a-ment, Jud-a-ment, Judg-a-ment day is a-rolling around." In "Oh, Rocks, Don't Fall on Me," we find, "In-a-that great judgment day." This extra syllable was used much more generally in the past than now. Its use is now confined to those who have survived from ante-bellum days and to those who live in the rural districts. Those in the cities and schools are paying less and less attention to it. Time is working a change. Has rhythm, this perfect beauty in movement, any real importance in creation? The rhythm of the planets as they encircle each other with paths of light; the rhythm of the seasons as they follow each other, each bringing its own peculiar beauty and life suggest at least that rhythm is an important principle in creation, and is essential to the harmony of the universe. That the life of the Negro is rhythmic is an uncommon blessing. It is an ever-increasing wealth of happiness.

Another peculiarity is the common and surprising use of ejaculations at the dictates of feeling. Such ejaculations take the form of "O Lord!" "Hallelujah!" "O Yes!" "SSing!" "Sing it, children," and are usually thrown in by the leader, but oftentimes by others, just as the spirit moves; but by whomever it is interjected there is no violence done to the rhythm, and the effect is electrical. Sometimes such an expression, though extemporaneous and spontaneous, is so fitting and effective that it becomes a part of the song. The particular one of these that is the most effective is the single word "sing." It is a sharp spur to the singers. On one occasion, while in chapel exercises at Fisk, the students were singing in a purposeless manner the song, "I Want to be Ready"—the leader in the genuine Negro way, without harming the rhythm, shouted, "Sing!" With a sparkle in every eye, with a buoyancy supreme, that student body burst forth with such a volume of spirited song as is seldom permitted one to hear more than once in a lifetime—in harmony like a well-attuned organ, in power like the rushing of many waters.

Another peculiarity is a certain subtle effect which only the true "Jubilee Voice" can produce. This is indescribable, for it consists in certain turns, twists, and intonations not represented by any musical term. To be appreciated, it must be heard.

In the "American History and Encyclopædia of Music" is found the following statement: "In order to form a true conception of Negro Songs it is necessary to hear them sung by their creators. For the Negro possesses a peculiar quality of voice which it is next to impossible to 'imitate.'" True, there is a "peculiar quality" in the Negro voice, which it is difficult if not "impossible" to "imitate"; but it is more than "quality of voice" which makes the Negro singing interesting; it is the use of the voice. This use of the voice is what gives that subtle, indescribable effect in some of the Folk Songs, which many find so fascinatingly strange. This effect is produced without conscious effort, it is only the natural expression of what the singer feels. Success in singing Negro Folk Song is dependent upon a certain spiritual condition, a religious state. The voice is not nearly so important as the spirit.

Of course, the ideal singer of this music is the one whose spiritual condition is deepest and whose voice is best. There are those whose minds as well as whose spirits, voices, and experience finely fit them for the satisfactory singing of this music. Among those who have almost perfected the art of "Jubilee Singing," Mrs. Ella Sheppard Moore of the Original Jubilee Singers, now of blessed memory, but who is still an inspiration to us who are studying Negro music; Mrs. Mabel Grant Hadley and Rev. James A. Myers, are prominent examples. Education and training have not taken from them that spirituality and courage necessary to a proper rendering of these songs. That quality as expressed in the ability to sing the folk song effectively is not prevalent among the educated Negroes, for it is considered bad musical taste by most of those who teach Negroes. This is because such teachers have no comprehension of the importance of race consciousness, or they have no understanding of the worth of the music. Some are, as yet, too thoroughly possessed of the classical idea, or too sensitive to the question of slavery to give serious study to this music, but the time is coming when the essentials of the Negro Folk Song will be the dominant forces in a new music. "The composer is yet to arise," states the History and Encyclopædia of Music, "who will take those bits of melody, typical of his race, and on them construct compositions of true artistic work."

Coledridge-Taylor has set a fine example in his transcriptions of Negro melodies. In fact, his example is worth more to the Negro race than what he accomplished in a musical way. His productions, based upon these melodies thematically, are most assuredly artistic. For one who knew nothing of the life and conditions of those who created these songs, he expressed their spirit remarkably well. This spirit is American, generated on the Southern plantations, and these melodies breathe out Southern life just as truly as the magnolia sheds its fragrance, or the mocking bird flutes his song. Again, let it be repeated that Coleridge-Taylor has given inspiration, a powerful force for progress, and this will certainly lead some Negro composer, possessed of the same spirit that vitalizes the Negro Folk Song, to give to the world productions throbbing with our own life forces and worthy to be bound in gold. "God hath given to every people a prophet in their own tongues," states the Koran. The spontaneous birth and consequent growth of this music are decidedly distinguishing features. It bursts out of hearts in a state of almost religious frenzy. At such times only the theme and probably a stanza were born; afterwards there are some developments as the new song is sung in different localities. In this spontaneity, the Folk Song of the American Negro stands preëminent. Go out among the rural churches to-day and attend the "Big Meetings," and there will spring up before your very eyes the first fresh shouts of songs which are soon to flourish and fructify. During slavery in some localities it was a custom to require each new convert, before allowing him to "join the church" to sing a new song, and many a passion flower of the slave cabin smiling through dewey tears, raised up its face, greeting the brightness of the sun.

Finally, the very foundation of this music is of the Negro's building. The scale is peculiarly his own, and consequently satisfies his nature. Through it this nature manifests itself to the world. The spirit of music is a common possession which takes outward form according to the nature of the possessor. The Negro in his primitive nature expressed his musical scale 1-2-3-5-6. Why? That was all the world meant to him. But the American Negro has gone one step further and added one more note, flat seven, an addition which goes a long way toward expressing the effect of added experience brought to him by a new life in a New World. This flat seven expresses a wild and overwhelming surprise at the utter strangeness of things. Who can describe the feelings of the African slave as he beheld this great American civilization unfolding itself? What are the feelings of an infant as the big world gradually opens up itself? What would be the feelings of a black boy who had been born and reared in a cabin of the black belt, if suddenly he should be placed in the palace of a king? Compared to the feelings of the African in the presence of this new American civilization, these are as the gentle ripple on the calm bosom of the lake to the boisterous billows of the deep. All this feeling of the African's awe was injected into that little flat seven, America's contribution to the Negro's scale.

The conditions and experiences which put this wild, strange note into the being of the American Negro, must have been supremely overpowering. They must have cut their way into the very springs of his life, for their influence is abiding. Careful investigation has shown that Negroes born since freedom who have made no study of the Folk Song, in fact, know nothing technical about it, will often unconsciously strike this note in songs in which it is not supposed to occur. While they are singing for the simple joy of it, that note will frequently peal out with its weirdness.

The Folk Song of the American Negro, then, is characterized by the elements of religion, rhythm, syncopation, spontaneity, and the sexatonic scale with the flat seven expressing surprise and the absence of any feeling of hatred or revenge.

Balm in Gilead.

There is a Balm in Gil-e-ad, To make the wounded whole, There is a Balm in Gil-e-ad, To heal the sin-sick soul. There is a soul.

1. Some-times I feel dis-cour-aged, And think my work's in vain, But then the Ho-ly Spir-it Re-vives my soul a-gain. There is a
2. Don't ev-er feel dis-cour-aged, For Je-sus is your friend, And if you lack for knowledge, He'll ne'er re-fuse to lend. There is a
3. If you can-not preach like Pe-ter, If you can-not pray like Paul, You can tell the love of Je-sus, And say, "He died for all." There is a

CHAPTER V.

NUMBER AND CLASSIFICATION.

"The object of music is to strengthen and ennoble the soul."

FROM the nature of the case it is impossible to state definitely the number of these songs; impossible even to approximate it. That they reach well up into the hundreds is evidenced by the books that have been published by Fisk, Hampton, Calhoun, and by individuals connected with no institution of learning. That their number is even larger is shown by the numerous "new" songs and fragments which we are continually discovering. There are songs which are practically never heard outside of the localities where they were born. Those interested in collecting this music, go into these localities and gather them. Collections of these songs are continually increased by the following contributing agencies:

(1) Students, new and old, coming to our schools year by year, bring them to us, (2) we, ourselves, passing from state to state falling in with older members of our race, and attending our churches which are still influenced by ante-bellum life, and find many a song we have never heard before. Many a time we find a song which we call "new," thinking that it was more lately born than those we know so well, but in most cases we find some person whose grandmother or grandfather used to sing it all the time, and sometimes we even find that very old grandmother or grandfather whose favorite it was. So now we never call a song "new" in point of its birth, but from the point of our acquaintance with it. After what deserves to be called a thorough investigation, we are led to the conclusion that practically all, if not absolutely all, of the best and most interesting of these songs were born in slavery days; the songs of the Negro produced since those days bear the marks of attempted composition, usually called "ballads," and are generally poor imitations. Sometimes we find one song to be practically two, which is a result of development or of mistaken interpretation, sometimes the same words to different tunes, or the same tune used with different words. The following are examples:

"I'm-a-goin' to do all I can for my Lord," which words are used with the same tune as "I've a mother in the kingdom, ain't that good news?" Almost the identical air is used to the following three sets of words:

(1) "Free at last, free at last; I thank God, I'm free at last."
(2) "Hold the wind, hold the wind; Hold the wind, don't let it blow."
(3) "Stand on the rock, Stand on the rock, Stand on the rock a little longer."

Conditions were favorable for the birth of a large number of songs. The Bible is the main source both of the subject, and material for the music. This in itself is an inexhaustible source. Then the different surroundings in different localities, influencing the imagination of the Negro, caused a diversity of thought and of connection, which in turn gave birth to a variety of songs. In the light of all these facts it is easy to understand how these songs would increase very rapidly and soon become as numerous as the stars, "a number that no man can number." While we must acknowledge a positive and absolute indefiniteness as to the number of these songs, in regard to classification we can state quite accurately where each song with which we are acquainted belongs. To begin with, there are two extremes of emotion,—joy and sorrow—expressed in this music. There is practically no middle ground. At first it seems strange that so little attention was given to the common every-day life, but then, when we recall that this work-a-day life had so few attractions, his strangeness disappears.

JOY SONGS.

"Great Camp Meeting."

1. Oh, walk together children; Don't you get a-weary;
   Walk together children; Don't you get a-weary;
   Walk together children; Don't you get a-weary;
   There's a great camp meeting in the promise land.

2. Oh, sing together children, Don't you get-a-weary,
   Sing together children, Don't you get-a-weary;
   Sing together children, Don't you get-a-weary;
   There's a great camp meeting in the promise land.

3. Going to moan and never tire,
   Moan and never tire,
   Moan and never tire,
   There's a great camp meeting in the promise land.

"Peter, Go Ring Them Bells."

Chorus

Oh, Peter, go ring them bells,
Peter, go ring them bells,
Peter, go ring them bells,
I heard from Heaven to-day.
Oh, I heard from Heaven to-day,
Heard from Heaven to-day,
Oh, thank God, and I thank you too,
I heard from Heaven to-day.

1. I wonder where sister Mary's gone,
   Wonder where sister Mary's gone,
   Wonder where sister Mary's gone,
   I heard from Heaven to-day.

Chorus

Oh, heard from Heaven to-day, etc.

"Free at Last."

Chorus

Oh, free at last, free at last,
I thank God I'm free at last,
Free at last, free at last,
I thank God I'm free at last.

1. Way down yonder in the graveyard walk,
   I thank God I'm free at last,
   Me and my Jesus goin' to meet and talk,
   I thank God I'm free at last.

Chorus

Oh, free at last, etc.

2. Down on my knees when the light passed by,
   I thank God I'm free at last,
   Thought my soul would rise and fly,
   I thank God I'm free at last.

Chorus

Oh, free at last, etc.

"WIDE RIVER."

Chorus

Oh, wasn't that a wide river,
   River of Jordan, Lord,
Wide river,
   There's one more river to cross.

1. Oh, the River of Jordan is so wide,
   One more river to cross,
And I don't know how to get on the other side,
   One more river to cross.

Chorus

Oh, wasn't that a wide river, etc.

2. Shout, shout, Satan's about,
   One more river to cross,
Shut your door and keep him out,
   One more river to cross.

Chorus

Oh, wasn't that a wide river, etc.

"SOME OF THESE MORNINGS."

1. Going to see my mother,
   Some o' these mornings,
See my mother,
   Some o' these mornings,
See my mother,
   Some o' these mornings,
Hope I'll join the band.

2. Going to chatter with the angels,
   Some o' these mornings,
Chatter with the angels,
   Some o' these mornings,
Chatter with the angels,
   Some o' these mornings,
Hope I'll join the band.

Chorus

Look away in the Heavens,
Look away in the Heavens,
Look away, in the Heavens, Lord;
Hope I'll join the band.

"Oh, Religion is a Fortune!"

Chorus

Oh, religion is a fortune,
   I really do believe,
Oh, religion is a fortune,
   I really do believe.

1. Where've you been, sister Mary,
   Where've you been so long,
   Been low down in the valley for to pray,
   And I ain't got weary yet.

Chorus

Oh, religion is a fortune, etc.

2. Where've you been, poor mourner,
   Where've you been so long,
   Been low down in the valley for to pray,
   And I ain't got weary yet.

Chorus

Oh, religion is a fortune, etc.

"Shout All Over God's Heaven."

1. I got a cross,
   You got a cross,
   All-a-God's children got a cross,
   When I get to Heaven,
   Goin' to lay down my cross,
   Goin' to shout all over God's Heaven,
   Heaven, Heaven.
   Everybody talking about Heaven ain't goin' there,
   Heaven, Heaven.
   Shout all over God's Heaven.

2. I got a song,
   You got a song,
   All-a-God's children got a song,
   When I get to Heaven,
   Goin' to sing a new song,
   Goin' to sing all over God's Heaven,
   Heaven, Heaven.
   Everybody talking about Heaven ain't goin' there,
   Heaven, Heaven.
   Sing all over God's Heaven.

NUMBER AND CLASSIFICATION.

"Good News, the Chariot's Coming."

Chorus

Good news, the chariot's coming,
Good news, the chariot's coming,
Good news, the chariot's coming,
And I don't want-her to leave-a-me behind.

1. It's a golden chariot,—Carry me home,
A golden chariot,—Carry me home,
A golden chariot,—Carry me home,
And I don't want-her to leave-a-me behind.

Chorus

Good news, the chariot's coming, etc.

2. There's a long white robe, In the heaven I know;
A long white robe,—In the heaven I know;
A long white robe,—In the heaven I know;
And I don't want-her to leave-a-me behind.

Chorus

Good news, the chariot's coming, etc.

"Rise, Shine, for Thy Light is-a-coming."

Chorus

Oh rise, shine, for thy light is-a-coming,
Oh rise, shine, for thy light is-a-coming,
Oh rise, shine, for thy light is-a-coming,
My Lord says He's coming by and by.

1. Oh wet and dry I intend to try,
    My Lord says He's coming by and by;
To serve the Lord until I die;
    My Lord says He's coming by and by.

Chorus

Oh rise, shine, for thy light is-a-coming, etc.

2. This is the year of Jubilee,
    My Lord says He's coming by and by,
The Lord has set His people free,
    My Lord says He's coming by and by.

Chorus

Oh rise, shine, for thy light is-a-coming, etc.

SORROW SONGS.

"KEEP ME FROM SINKING DOWN."

Chorus

Oh Lord, Oh my Lord,
Oh Lord, Oh my Lord,
Keep me from sinking down.

1. I tell you what I mean to do,
    Keep me from sinking down.
   I mean to go to heaven, too,
    Keep me from sinking down.

Chorus

Oh Lord, Oh my Lord, etc.

2. I'm sometimes up, I'm sometimes down,
    Keep me from sinking down.
   Sometimes I'm level with the ground,
    Keep me from sinking down.

Chorus

Oh Lord, Oh my Lord, etc.

"NOBODY KNOWS THE TROUBLE I SEE."

Refrain

Nobody knows the trouble I see, Lord,
Nobody knows the trouble I see.
Nobody knows the trouble I see, Lord,
Nobody knows but Jesus.

1. Mother, won't you pray for me;
   Mother, won't you pray for me;
   Mother, won't you pray for me;
   And help me to drive old Satan away.

Refrain

Nobody knows the trouble I see, Lord, etc.

2. Preacher, won't you pray for me;
   Preacher, won't you pray for me;
   Preacher, won't you pray for me;
   And help me to drive old Satan away.

Refrain

Nobody knows the trouble I see, Lord, etc.

"Were You There When They Crucified My Lord?"

1. Were you there when they crucified my Lord?
   Were you there when they crucified my Lord?
      Oh, sometimes it causes me to tremble,—tremble,—tremble,
   Were you there when they crucified my Lord?

2. Were you there when they pierced Him in the side?
   Were you there when they pierced Him in the side?
      Oh, sometimes it causes me to tremble,—tremble,—tremble,
   Were you there when they pierced Him in the side?

3. Were you there when they laid Him in the tomb?
   Were you there when they laid Him in the tomb?
      Oh, sometimes it causes me to tremble,—tremble,—tremble,
   Were your there when they laid Him in the tomb?

"I'm Troubled in Mind."

Refrain
I'm troubled, I'm troubled, I'm troubled in mind;
And if Jesus don't help me, I surely will die.

1. When through the deep waters of trouble I go,
   The billows of sorrow cannot overflow.

   Refrain
   I'm troubled, etc.

2. Oh, come here, my Jesus, and help me along,
   Till up in bright glory, I sing a new song.

   Refrain
   I'm troubled, etc.

"Couldn't Hear Nobody Pray."

Chorus
I couldn't hear nobody pray,
Oh, I couldn't hear nobody pray,
Oh, way down yonder by myself,
And I couldn't hear nobody pray.

1. In the valley—Couldn't hear nobody pray;
   On-a my knees—Couldn't hear nobody pray;
   So lonesome—Couldn't hear nobody pray;
   With my burden—Couldn't hear nobody pray.

Chorus

And I couldn't hear nobody pray, etc.

2. Hallelujah—Couldn't hear nobody pray;
   Troubles over—Couldn't hear nobody pray;
   In the Kingdom—Couldn't hear nobody pray;
   With my Jesus—Couldn't hear nobody pray.

    Chorus

   And I couldn't hear nobody pray, etc.

"BEFORE THIS TIME ANOTHER YEAR."

Refrain

Before this time another year;
I may be gone,
Out in some lonesome graveyard,
Oh, Lord, how long?

1. My mother's took her flight and gone;
   Oh, Lord, how long?
   By the grace of God I'll follow on,
   Oh, Lord, how long?

    Refrain

   Before this time another year, etc.

2. My sister's took her flight and gone,
   Oh, Lord, how long?
   By the grace of God I'll follow on,
   Oh, Lord, how long?

    Refrain

   Before this time another year, etc.

"FAREWELL, MY DEAR MOTHER."

Refrain

Farewell, my dear mother;
Farewell, my dear mother;
Farewell, my dear mother;
Mother, mother, mother, mother!

1. For now I must leave you,
   Now I must leave you;
   Oh, now I must leave you,
   Leave you, leave you, leave you, leave you.

2. I'll meet you in heaven;
   I'll meet you in heaven;
   I'll meet you in heaven;
   Heaven, Heaven, Heaven, Heaven!

"Oh, Wretched Man that I Am."

Chorus

Oh, wretched man that I am;
Oh, wretched man that I am;
Oh, wretched man that I am;
   Who will deliver poor me?

1. I'm bowed down with a burden of woe,
   I'm bowed down with a burden of woe,
   I'm bowed down with a burden of woe,
   Who will deliver poor me?

   Chorus

   Oh, wretched man that I am, etc.

2. My heart's filled with sadness and pain,
   My heart's filled with sadness and pain,
   My heart's filled with sadness and pain,
   Who will deliver poor me?

"I Must Walk My Lonesome Valley."

1. I've got to walk my lonesome valley,
      I've got to walk it for myself;
   Nobody else can walk it for me,
      I've got to walk it for myself.

2. Jesus walked His lonesome valley,
      He had to walk it for Himself;
   Nobody else could walk it for Him;
      He had to walk it for Himself.

3. I've got to go and stand my trial,
      I've got to stand it for myself;
   Nobody else can stand it for me,
      I've got to stand it for myself.

4. Jesus had to stand His trial,
      He had to stand it for Himself;
   Nobody else could stand it for Him,
      He had to stand it for Himself.

"Feel Like a Motherless Child."

Chorus

I feel like, I feel like a motherless child,
I feel like, I feel like a motherless child,
I feel like, I feel like a motherless child,
Glory Hallelujah!

1. I have some friends before me gone,
   Glory Hallelujah!
   By the Grace of God I'll follow on,
   Glory Hallelujah!

Chorus

I feel like, I feel like a motherless child—

2. Sometimes my way is sad and lone,
   Glory Hallelujah!
   I'm far away and lost from home,
   Glory Hallelujah!

Chorus

I feel like, I feel like a motherless child—

"Live a Humble."

Chorus

Live a humble, humble,
Humble yourself.
The bells done rung,
Live a humble, humble,
Humble yourself.
The bells done rung.

1. You see God, you see God,
   You see God 'n the morning,
   He'll come a-riding down the line of time,
   Fire'll be falling, He'll be calling,
   Come to judg-a-ment-a-come.

Chorus

Live a humble, humble, etc.

2. Oh, the bells done rung,
   And the songs done sung,
   And a-don't let it catch you with your work undone.

Chorus

Live a humble, humble, etc.

The fertile imagination of the Negro was ever transporting his soul to the mount of ecstacy or into the valley of sorrow. While there is a plaintiveness running through all the songs, the emotion of joy is predominant. There is sometimes a triumphant "hallelujah" even in the valley. Truly the maker of these songs was he "who passing through the Valley of Baca maketh it a well."

The happiness of the Negro is truly proverbial, so it would be most unnatural if his songs were not laden with joy, and it is quite significant that this note of joy rises high and clear above the sobs and sighs crushed out of his heart. The Negro passes most of his life on the mountain top. He verifies the legend which describes him as the man of light and the son of the morning. His capacity for joy and its complement in his capacity for sorrow. No sorrow can be deeper; he drains the cup of suffering; he descends into the depths of the valley. But sorrow and suffering have not embittered him, nor have they taken away "the joys that sweeten life."

Mark Twain tells the story of an old negro servant of his, who seemed always to be happy. Her face was ever lighted with a smile and she shed a brightness wherever she went. "She was sixty years old, but her eye was undimmed and her strength unimpaired. It was no more trouble for her to laugh than for a bird to sing." "Aunt Rachel, how is it that you've lived sixty years and have had no trouble?" She told the story of her life. Of course, she had been a slave. She once had as happy a family as a slave could have. She had seen her husband and six children sold from her in one day. She saw them carried away into different directions, some away down South; and only one of whom, a boy, she had ever seen or heard of since. And yet, as Mark Twain says, "it was no more trouble for her to laugh than for a bird to sing." Aunt Rachel is an epitome of her race. She lives at the mountain top.

SORROW SONGS WITH NOTE OF JOY.

"WALK THROUGH THE VALLEY."

Refrain
We shall walk through the valley and the shadow of death,
　　We shall walk through the valley in peace;
If Jesus Himself shall be our leader,
　　We shall walk through the valley in peace.

1. We shall meet our loved ones there,
   We shall meet our loved ones there,
   If Jesus Himself shall be our leader,
   We shall walk through the valley in peace.

   Refrain

   We shall walk through the valley and the shadow of death, etc.

2. We shall meet our Saviour there,
   We shall meet our Saviour there,
   If Jesus Himself shall be our leader,
   We shall walk through the valley in peace.

   Refrain

   We shall walk through the valley and the shadow of death, etc.

"SOON-A-WILL BE DONE-A-WITH TROUBLES OF THE WORLD."

Chorus

Soon-a-will be done-a-with the troubles of the world,
Troubles of the World;
Soon-a-will be done-a-with the troubles of the world,
Goin' home to live with God.

1. These are my Father's children,
   These are my Father's children,
   These are my Father's children,
   All in-a-one band.

   Chorus

   Soon-a-will be done-a-with the troubles of the world, etc.

2. No more weeping and a-wailing,
   No more weeping and-awailing,
   No more weeping and-awailing,
   All in-a-one band.

   Chorus

   Soon-a-will be done-a-with the troubles of the world, etc.

"OH, MY LITTLE SOUL'S GOING TO SHINE."

Chorus

Oh, my little soul's going to shine, shine;
Oh, my little soul's going to shine, shine;
Oh, my little soul's going to shine, shine;
Oh, my little soul's going to shine, shine.

1. I'm going to tell God all-a-my troubles,
   I'm going to tell God all-a-my troubles,
   I'm going to tell God all-a-my troubles,
   Oh, my little soul's going to shine, shine;
   Oh, my little soul's going to shine, shine.

2. You may bury my body in the east of the garden,
   Bury my body in the east of the garden,
   Bury my body in the east of the garden,
   Oh, my little soul's going to shine, shine;
   Oh, my little soul's going to shine, shine.

"ALL OVER THIS WORLD."

Chorus
All over this world,
All over this world,
All over this world,
All over this world.

1. All-a-my troubles will soon be over with,
   Soon be over with, soon be over with,
   All-a-my troubles will soon be over with,
   All over this world.

Chorus
All over this world, etc.

2. All back sliding will soon be over with,
   Soon be over with, soon be over with,
   All back sliding will soon be over with,
   All over this world.

Chorus
All over this world, etc.

"OH, NOBODY KNOWS THE TROUBLE I SEE."

Chorus
Oh, nobody knows the trouble I see,
Nobody knows but Jesus.
Oh, nobody knows the trouble I see,
Glory hallelujah.

1. Sometimes I'm up,
   Sometimes I'm down,
   Oh, yes, Lord.
   Sometimes I'm level with the ground.
   Oh, yes, Lord.

Chorus

Oh, nobody knows the trouble I see, etc.

2. If you get there before I do,
   Oh, yes, Lord.
   Tell all-a-my friends I'm coming, too,
   Oh, yes, Lord.

Chorus

Oh, nobody knows the trouble I see, etc.

"Don't You Grieve for Me."

1. My sister's took her flight,
      And gone home,
      And the angel's waiting at the door;
   My sister's took her flight,
      And gone home,
      And the angel's waiting at the door.

Chorus

Tell all-a-my Father's children,
   Don't you grieve for me;
Tell all-a-my Father's children,
   Don't you grieve for me.

2. She has taken up her crown,
      And gone home,
      And the angel's waiting at the door;
   She has taken up her crown,
      And gone home,
      And the angel's waiting at the door.

Chorus

Tell all-a-my Father's children, etc.

"Oh, Rocks Don't Fall on Me."

Chorus

Oh, rocks don't fall on me,
Oh, rocks don't fall on me,
Oh, rocks don't fall on me,
Rocks and mountains don't fall on me.

1. Look over yonder on Jericho's walls,
    Rocks and mountains don't fall on me,
   See those sinners tremble and fall,
    Rocks and mountains don't fall on me.

   Chorus
   Oh, rocks don't fall on me, etc.

2. In-a that great, great judg-a-ment day,
    Rocks and mountains don't fall on me,
   The sinner will run to the rocks and say,
    Rocks and mountains please fall on me.

   Chorus
   Oh, rocks please fall on me, etc.

"Now We Take this Feeble Body."

1. Now we take this feeble body,
   And we carry it to the tomb,
   And we all leave it there,—Hallelujah.

   Chorus
   And a hallelujah,—And a hallelujah,
   And we all leave it there,—Hallelujah.

2. Now we take our dear old father,
   And we carry him to the tomb,
   And we all leave him there,—Hallelujah.

   Chorus
   And a hallelujah,—And a hallelujah—

"Swing Low, Sweet Chariot."

Chorus
Swing low, sweet chariot,,
 Coming for to carry me home;
Swing low, sweet chariot,
 Coming for to carry me home.

1. If you get there before I do,
    Coming for to carry me home;
   Tell all my friends I'm coming, too,
    Coming for to carry me home.

Chorus

Swing low, sweet chariot, etc.

2. I looked over Jordan and what did I see?
   Coming for to carry me home;
   A band of angels coming after me,
   Coming for to carry me home.

Chorus

Swing low, sweet chariot, etc.

"SOMEBODY'S BURIED IN THE GRAVEYARD."

Chorus

Somebody's buried in the graveyard,
   Somebody's buried in the sea;
Going to get up in the morning a-shouting,
   Going to sound Jubilee.

1. Sometimes I'm up, sometimes I'm down,
   But still my soul feels Heavenly bound.

Chorus

Somebody's buried in the graveyard,
   Somebody's buried in the sea;
Going to get up in the morning a-shouting,
   Going to sound Jubilee.

A further classification presents a more interesting phase. The songs group themselves under Faith, Hope, Love, Determination, Adoration, Patience, Courage, and Humility.

SONGS OF FAITH.

"YOU MAY BURY ME IN THE EAST."

1. You may bury me in the East,
   You may bury me in the West,
   But I'll hear the trumpet sound,
   In-a that morning.

Refrain

In-a that morning,
How I long to go,
For to hear the trumpet sound,
In-a that morning.

2. In-a that dreadful judg-a-ment day,
We'll take wings and fly away,
For to hear the trumpet sound,
In-a that morning.

Refrain

In-a that morning, etc.

"All I Want is a Little More Faith."

Chorus

All I want,
All I want,
All I want,
Is a little more faith in Jesus.

1. Did ever you see such a man as God,
A little more faith in Jesus,
A preaching the gospel to the poor,
A little more faith in Jesus.

Chorus

It's all I want, etc.

2. He died for all upon the tree,
A little more faith in Jesus;
He died for you and He died for me,
A little more faith in Jesus.

Chorus

Oh, it's all I want, etc.

"I Have Another Building."

Chorus

I know I have another building,
I know it's not made with hands;
I know I have another building,
I know it's not made with hands.

1. I haven't been to Heaven,
     But I've been told,
   Not made with hands,
   That the streets are pearl
     And the gates are gold;
   Not made with hands.

   Chorus

   I know I have another building, etc.

2. Some of these morning bright and fair,
     Not made with hands;
   Going to meet my Jesus in-a-the air;
     Not made with hands.

   Chorus

   I know I have another building, etc.

SONGS OF HOPE.

"In Bright Mansions Above."

Chorus

In bright mansions above,
In bright mansions above,
Lord, I want to live up yonder,
In bright mansions above.

1. My mother's gone to glory,
   I want to go there, too;
   Lord, I want to live up yonder,
   In bright mansions above.

   Chorus

   In bright mansions above, etc.

2. My Saviour's gone to glory,
   I want to go there, too;
   Lord, I want to live up yonder,
   In bright mansions above.

   Chorus

   In bright mansions above, etc.

"Good Lord, When I Die."

Chorus

Good Lord, when I die,
Good Lord, when I die,
Good Lord, when I die, shout one,
Good Lord, when I die.

1. I want to go to Heaven
   When I die.
   I want to go to Heaven
   When I die.
   I want to go to Heaven
   When I die.
   Good Lord, when I die.

   Chorus

   Good Lord, when I die, etc.

2. Oh, I want to see my Jesus,
   When I die.
   I want to see my Jesus,
   When I die.
   I want to see my Jesus,
   When I die.
   Good Lord, when I die.

   Chorus

   Good Lord, when I die, etc.

"I Hope I'll Join the Band."

1. Ride up in the chariot,
       Soon-a in the morning,
   Ride up in the chariot,
       Soon-a in the morning,
   Ride up in the chariot,
       Soon-a in the morning,
   And I hope I'll join the band.

   Chorus

   Oh, Lord, have mercy on me,
   Oh, Lord, have mercy on me,
   Oh, Lord, have mercy on me,
   And I hope I'll join the band.

2. Going to chatter with the angels,
    Soon-a in the morning,
   Chatter with the angels,
    Soon-a in the morning,
   Chatter with the angels,
    Soon-a in the morning,
   And I hope I'll join the band.

Chorus

Oh, Lord, have mercy on me, etc.

SONGS OF LOVE.

"I Know the Lord's Laid His Hands on Me."

Chorus

Oh, I know the Lord,
I know the Lord,
I know the Lord has laid His hands on me.

1. I'm born of God I know I am,
    I know the Lord has laid His hands on me,
   Been new born by the dying Lamb,
    I know the Lord has laid His hands on me.

Chorus

Oh, I know the Lord, etc.

2. He took me from the miry clay,
    I know the Lord has laid His hands on me,
   And told me to walk the narrow way,
    I know the Lord has laid His hands on me.

Chorus

Oh, I know the Lord, etc.

3. I never felt such love before,
    I know the Lord has laid His hands on me,
   Saying, "Go in peace and sin no more,"
    I know the Lord has laid His hands on me.

Chorus

Oh, I know the Lord, etc.

"Love Come Twinkling Down."

Chorus

Oh, the love come twinkling down,
Oh, the love come twinkling down,
Oh, the love come twinkling down,
Oh, the love come twinkling down.

1. All around me,
    The love come twinkling down,
   From-a-heaven,
    The love come twinkling down.

Chorus

Oh, the love come twinkling down, etc.

2. Help me Jesus,
    Love come twinkling down,
   Pity Lord,
    Love come twinkling down.

Chorus

Oh, the love come twinkling down, etc.

"Old Time Religion."

Chorus

Give me this-a-old time religion,
Give me this-a-old time religion,
Give me this-a-old time religion,
    It's good enough for me.

1. It was good for my old mother,
   It was good for my old mother,
   It was good for my old mother,
       It's good enough for me.

Chorus

Give me this-a-old time religion, etc.

2. Makes me love everybody,
   Makes me love everybody,
   Makes me love everybody,
       It's good enough for me.

Chorus

Give me this-a-old time religion, etc.

SONGS OF DETERMINATION.

"Oh, Yes, I'm Going Up."

Chorus

Oh, yes, I'm going up, going up,
    Going all the way, Lord.
Going up, going up,
    To see the heavenly land.

1. I'm going up to heaven for to see my robe,
    See the heavenly land.
Going to see my robe and try it on,
    See the heavenly land.
It's brighter than the glittering sun,
    See the heavenly land.
Oh, saints and sinners will-a-you go,
    See the heavenly land.

Chorus

Oh, yes, I'm going up, etc.

2. I tell you what I like-a-the best,
    See the heavenly land.
It is them shouting Methodist,
    See the heavenly land.
They shout so loud that the Devil looks,
    See the heavenly land.
And he gets away with his cloven foot,
    See the heavenly land.

Chorus

Oh, yes, I'm going up, etc.

"Keep-a-Inching Along."

Chorus

Keep-a-inching along,
Keep-a-inching along,
Jesus will come by and by,
Keep-a-inching along, like a poor inch worm,
Jesus will come by and by.

1. 'Twas inch by inch I sought the Lord,
    Jesus will come by and by;
   'Twas inch by inch I found His word,
    Jesus will come by and by.

   Chorus

   Keep-a-inching along, etc.

2. Down on my knees when the light passed by,
    Jesus will come by and by;
   I though my soul would rise and fly,
    Jesus will come by and by.

   Chorus

   Keep-a-inching along, etc.

"Made My Vow to the Lord."

Refrain

Done made my vow to the Lord,
And I never will turn back,
I will go, I shall go,
To see what the end will be.

1. My strength, Good Lord, is almost gone,
   I will go; I shall go,
   To see what the end will be,
   But you have told me to press on,
   I will go, I shall go,
   To see what the end will be.

   Refrain

   Done made my vow to the Lord, etc.

2. Sometimes I'm helpless on the ground,
   I will go, I shall go,
   To see what the end will be,
   But Jesus speaks and I'm heavenly bound,
   I will go, I shall go,
   To see what the end will be.

   Refrain

   Done made my vow to the Lord, etc.

SONGS OF ADORATION.

"HE IS KING OF KINGS."

Chorus

He is King of Kings,
He is Lord of Lords,
Jesus Christ the first and the last,
No man-a-works like Him.

1. He sets His throne in the middle of the air,
    No man works like Him,
    And sends His angels everywhere,
    No man works like Him.

Chorus

He is King of Kings, etc.

2. He sends them east and He sends them west,
    No man works like Him,
    He tells them give His people rest,
    No man works like Him.

Chorus

He is King of Kings, etc.

"KING EMANUEL."

1. Oh, who do call King Emanuel,
    I call my Jesus King Emanuel.

Chorus

Oh, de King Emanuel is a mighty Emanuel,
I call my Jesus King Emanuel.

2. Oh, some call Him Jesus,
    But I call Him Lord,
    I call my Jesus King Emanuel;
    Let's talk about de heaven and de heaven's fine things,
    I call my Jesus King Emanuel.

Chorus

Oh, de King Emanuel is a mighty Emanuel,
I call my Jesus King Emanuel.

"Love King Jesus."

Chorus

Elder, you say you love King Jesus;
Elder, you say you love the Lord.

1. Oh, come and let us know,
    How you love King Jesus;
  Come and let us know,
    How you love the Lord.

Chorus

Sister, you say you love King Jesus;
Sister, you say you love the Lord.

2. Oh, sing and let us know how you love King Jesus,
  Sing and let us know how you love the Lord.

Chorus

Children, you say you love King Jesus;
Children, you say you love the Lord.

SONGS OF PATIENCE.

"Wait a Little While."

Chorus

Wait a little while,
  Then we'll sing the new song,
Wait a little while,
  Then we'll sing the new song.

1. My heavenly home is bright and fair,
    Then we'll sing the new song,
  No pain or sorrow over there,
    Then we'll sing the new song.

Chorus

Wait a little while, etc.

2. Sometimes I get a heavenly view,
    Then we'll sing the new song,
  And then my trials are so few,
    Then we'll sing the new song.

Chorus

Wait a little while, etc.

"Mighty Rocky Road."

1. It's a mighty rocky road,
    Most done traveling,
   Mighty rocky road,
    Most done traveling,
   Mighty rocky road,
    Most done traveling,
   Bound to carry my soul to the Lord.

   Chorus

   I'm bound to carry my soul to Jesus,
    Bound to carry my soul to the Lord,
   I'm bound to carry my soul to Jesus,
    Bound to carry my soul to the Lord.

2. My sister's on the road,
    Most done traveling,
   Sister's on the road,
    Most done traveling,
   Sister's on the road,
    Most done traveling,
   Bound to carry my soul to the Lord.

   Chorus

   I'm bound to carry my soul to Jesus, etc.

"By and By."

Chorus

Oh, by and by, by and by,
I'm a-going to lay down my heavy load.

1. I know my robe's going to fit a-me, well.
    I'm a-going to lay down my heavy load;
   I tried it on at the gates of hell,
    I'm a-going to lay down my heavy load.

   Chorus

   Oh, by and by, by and by, etc.

2. Oh, some-a these mornings bright and fair,
    I'm a-going to lay down my heavy load;
   Going to take-a my wings and cleave the air,
    I'm a-going to lay down my heavy load.

   Chorus

   Oh, by and by, by and by, etc.

SONGS OF COURAGE.

"March On."

Chorus

March on and you shall gain the victory,
March on and you shall gain the day.

1. We want no cowards in our day,
   You shall gain the victory.
   We call for valiant-hearted men,
   You shall gain the day.

Chorus

March on and you shall gain the victory, etc.

2. This is the year of Jubilee,
   You shall gain the victory,
   The Lord has set His people free,
   You shall gain the day.

Chorus

March on and you shall gain the victory, etc.

"Stay in the Field."

Chorus

Stay in the field,
Stay in the field,
Stay in the field,
Until the war is ended.

1. Mine eyes are turned to the Heavenly gate,
   Till the war is ended.
   I'll keep my way, or I'll be too late,
   Till the war is ended.

Chorus

Stay in the field, etc.

2. Green trees burning, why not the dry?
   Till the war is ended.
   My Saviour died, Oh, why not I?
   Till the war is ended.

SONGS OF HUMILITY.

"Reign, Oh, Reign."

Chorus
Oh, reign, Oh, reign,
  Oh, reign my Saviour,
Reign, Master Jesus, reign,
  Oh, reign salvation in my poor soul,
Reign, Master Jesus, reign.

1. I tell you now as I told you before,
    Reign, Master Jesus, reign,
   To the promise land I'm bound to go,
    Reign, Master Jesus, reign.

Chorus
Oh, reign, Oh, reign, etc.

2. I never shall forget that day,
    Reign, Master Jesus, reign,
   When Jesus washed my sin's away,
    Reign, Master Jesus, reign.

Chorus
Oh, reign, Oh, reign, etc.

The very few songs that do not come under any one of these heads as already given are represented by such songs as: "Ole Ark," "Little David." It is likely that the majority of the stanzas of these songs not originally composed, belong to them. It is a fact that the stanza in "Little David"—"I tell you once," etc.,—was a contribution from a student of Fisk University. The chorus of each of these songs is evidently genuine.

"THE OLE ARK."

Chorus

Oh, the ole ark's a-movering, movering, movering,
The ole ark's a-movering,
And I'm going home.
The ole ark she reel,
The ole ark she rock,
The ole ark she landed on the mountain top,
Oh, the ole ark's a-movering, movering, movering,
The ole ark's a-movering,
And I'm going home.

1. You see that sister dress so fine,
   She ain't got Jesus in her mind.

   Chorus
   Oh, the ole ark's a-movering, etc.

2. There ain't but the one thing grieve my mind,
   Sister's gone to heaven and a-left me behind.

   Chorus
   Oh, the ole ark's a-movering, etc.

"LITTLE DAVID."

Chorus

Little David play on your harp,
    Hallelu', hallelu'.
Little David play on your harp,
    Hallelu'.

1. Joshua was the son of Nun,
   He never would quit, till the work was done.

   Chorus
   Little David play on your harp, etc.

2. I tell you once, I tell you twice,
   There are sinners in hell for shooting dice.

   Chorus
   Little David play on your harp, etc.

"LIVE A HUMBLE."

Chorus

Live a humble, humble,
Humble yourself,
The bells done rung.
Live a humble, humble,
Humble yourself,
The bells done rung.

1. You see God, you see God,
   You see God 'n the morning,
   He'll come a-riding down the line of time,
   Fire'll be falling, He'll be calling,
   Come to judg-a-ment-a-come.

Chorus

Live a humble, humble, etc.

2. Oh, the bells done rung,
   And the songs done sung,
   And-a don't let it catch you with your work undone.

Chorus

Live a humble, humble, etc.

"BOW LOW, ELDER."

Chorus

Bow low, Elder,
  Jesus lis-a-ning,
Bow low, Elder,
  Jesus died.

1. When you see me on my knees,
   Raise me, Jesus, if-a you please.

Chorus

Bow low, Elder, etc.

2. When you see my coffin come,
   Then a-you know my soul's gone home.

Chorus

Bow low, Elder, etc.

The number of these songs is practically unknown; in classification they are positive, definite and satisfying.

* THIS IS A SIN-TRYING WORLD

LEADER: O, Lord!

CHORUS: O, this is a sin-try-ing world, This is a sin-try-ing world, This is a sin-try-ing world,

Help me, Jesus!

Sing it, children!

world, This is a sin-try-ing world. FINE.

1. O Heav'n is so high, and I am so low,
2. ※ Jordan's stream is chilly and wide,
3. ※ Way over yonder in the harvest fields,
4. You may bury me in the East, you may bury me in the West,

I don't know whether I'll ever get to Heav'n or no......
None can...... cross but the sanc-ti-fied......
The an-gels...... shov-ing at the char-i-ot wheels.
But in that...... morning my soul will be at rest......

Exclamations for Verses

1. High Heaven!	2. Cold Jordan!	3. O the harvest!	4. In the Heavens!
Hard trials!	Deep and wide!	Few laborers!	With my mother!
Crown of Life!	Can't you cross it?	Won't you join them?	And my Saviour!

CHAPTER VI.

BIRTH AND GROWTH OF CERTAIN SONGS, WITH EXPOSITION.

"Music is a fair and glorious gift of God;
I would not for the world, renounce my humble share in Music."

IN a general way, we know how this music as a whole was produced; that is, the conditions and forces which gave it birth. Facts and theories have been presented in foregoing chapters. The vagueness and uncertainty surrounding its beginning clothe it in a fascinating mystery, imparting an aspect of the supernatural. In the cases of some individual songs, however, we have definite and accurate knowledge of birth and growth. Parts of the history of some songs are so extraordinary that many receive them "cum grano salis," but even in these instances it is morally certain the events occurred as narrated. Many of these melodies had their birth during the seasons of religious meetings. Masters generally granted the privilege of holding such meetings, for they had a certain degree of faith in the slave's religion. It made him a better slave and kept his mind from plottings. Sometimes the overseer was present, sometimes not. Sometimes the slave was even allowed to attend the master's church. The slave's soul demanded communion with God quite as unfailingly as his body demanded food. Some masters, however, did not believe either in the slave's religion or his God.

Some masters who did not believe in the slave's God or in his religion had some extraordinary experiences. In Southern Kentucky, a slave, John by name, was known for his piety, religion, and seasons of prayer and praise. Like Daniel in Babylon, nothing could prevent him from turning his face toward Jerusalem in prayer. The time came when John had to be sold. The master who was about to buy him said, "John, they tell me that you are one of these great praying niggers. Now, I want to tell you that when I buy you, all that stuff must stop." ,"As a heart unspotted is not easily daunted," John answered, "Massa, ef dat's de case, you better not buy me, for I'se boun' to pray, and I'se goin' to pray." "All right, we'll see about that," said the master, and John was bought. It was not long before this master missed John, and upon learning from the slave's own lips that he had been praying, his wrath blazed in angry flame, and with curses he tore John's flesh with the cruel lash. He did his best to kill him. That night, the master lay down in complacency, while John lay down in torture. But peace and complacency soon flew away on the dark wings of the night, and the master was troubled in mind. His soul was like the stormy sea. He left his bed and walked the floor. The love of a wife could not comfort him, and the physician he refused to see, for the physician could not reach his case. The God of John and of John's religion had convicted the master of his sinfulness. When no help came to his tempestuous soul, in his extremity he said, "Send for John." With labored step, John struggled to the big house with a prayer upon his lips, and when the master saw him, he cried, "John, pray for me." In bloody pain, John sank down upon his knees and prayed for his weeping master, that his sins might be forgiven, and his soul made white in the blood of the Lamb! God heard that prayer, and the light of a new life broke in upon the master's vision. "Redeemed!" he cried. In reference to John, the remainder of the master's life was expressed in these words, "The best investment I ever made, the best money I ever spent, was when I bought John." John was cast into the den of lions, but they harmed him not.

On a plantation down on the Red River, in the early part of the nineteenth century, a master of a large number of slaves was accustomed to allow them to go across the river, at stated times, that they might worship with the Indians, who had a mission there. Upon the days of these services, the slaves crossed the river in many an ingenious craft. They always enjoyed themselves, and talked much of the good times on the other side. But one day the master learned that the missionary to the Indians was a northern man; and, believing that he might put ideas of freedom in the heads of his slaves, even if "in a Bibleistic way," as Dunbar says, which might lead them to travel the nightly path toward the North Star, he forthwith pursued the logical course and prohibited his slaves from worshiping any more across the river. Doubtless the master thought the matter was settled then and there, but not so; the slaves could not forget the good times across the river; and what they could not do in the open they determined to do in secret. They decided to "steal away to Jesus," as one slave expressed it. "Steal away to Jesus," whispered at first, later chanted softly, was notice that that night there were to be services across the river. The first-born thought, "Steal away to Jesus," was expressed all day, in the fields of cotton and of corn, and in fragments of tuneful melody the slaves were all informed of what would occur that night. At night when the master, overseer, and hounds had retired to sweet sleep, the slaves would steal from their cabins and quietly creep through the cotton, corn, and tall grasses, softly humming their greetings to one another. On toward the river they crept, and the night breezes wafted their melody to the ears of the missionary, who thereby knew that his black congregation was coming. Soon he espied here, there, and yonder, black forms, on rafts secretly made for the purpose, paddling themselves across the river. When they reached the banks, they lifted their voices in lofty inspiration, and from the depths of their hearts sang:

"My Lord, He calls me. He calls me by de thunder;
De trumpet soun's it in-a my soul;
I ain't got long to stay here."

The trees swaying in the night wind inspired them to proclaim, "Green trees a-bendin', poor sinner stands a-tremblin', de trumpet soun's it in a-my soul, I ain't got long to stay here." The judgment day, the most important day in his calendar, impressed itself upon him—

"Tombstones a-bustin',
Poor sinner stands a-tremblin',
De trumpet soun's it in-a my soul."

Of course, this song as we have it to-day was not produced in one night; it is a product of development, for the missionary who told the story to the Original Fisk Jubilee Singers, stated that he literally saw the song grow. Each stanza, as well as the chorus, ends with the expression, "I ain't got long to stay here," which was not originally sacred, but a sharp reminder to the slaves that they must not stay too long on that side of the river, or they must pay the penalty of disobeying their master. Too well they knew what such a penalty would be. So that little expression had to them a tremendous meaning.

"Swing Low, Sweet Chariot" and "Before I'd be a Slave," upon first hand authority, may be called the "Twins," for they burst from

MRS. SARAH HANNAH SHEPPARD,

In whose heart was born "Swing Low, Sweet Chariot" and "Before I'd be a Slave, I'd be Buried in My Grave."

the same soul of anguish. These songs were born from the same heart at the same time and under the same condition.

> "Before I'd be a slave,
> I'd be buried in my grave,
> And a-don't let it catch you with your work undone.

A master of a Tennessee plantation had sold a mother from her babe, and the day for the separation was fast approaching when the mother was to be taken "down South." Now, the condition of the slave in Tennessee was better than that in any other state, with the possible exception of Virginia. To be sold "South" was, to the slave, to make the journey from which no traveler ever returned. So it was not strange that the mother would sooner take her life and that of her babe, than to go down into Mississippi, which, to her, was going to her grave. Bent upon throwing herself and her child over the steep banks of the Cumberland River, she was stumbling along the dusty road, her infant clasped close to her breast, muttering in frenzy her dire determination, "Before I'd be a slave, I'd be buried in my grave!" An old "mammy," seeing the terrible expression on her face, and hearing these words, read her intentions. In love she laid her dear old hand upon the shoulder of the distressed mother and said, "Don't you do it, honey; wait, let de chariot of de Lord swing low, and let me take one of de Lord's scrolls an' read it to you." Then, making a motion as reaching for something, and unrolling it, she read, "God's got a great work for dis baby to do; she's goin' to stand befo' kings and queens. Don't you do it, honey." The mother was so impressed with the words of the old "mammy" she gave up her fell design and allowed herself to be taken off down into Mississippi, leaving her baby behind. These two songs grew by degrees, as they passed from mouth to mouth, until they reached their present state. That prophecy of the old "mammy" was literally fulfilled. After the war, the baby girl entered Fisk University and was a member of the Original Fisk Jubilee Singers, who stood before kings and queens. When the tour of the singers was ended, this girl set out to find her mother, and after searching for some time, found her and brought her into a beautiful home, where she lived in love and comfort until the summer of 1912, when "the Sweet Chariot Swung Low" and bore her home. She had been unconscious for some hours, but when she heard the strains of this, her heart-born song, which was

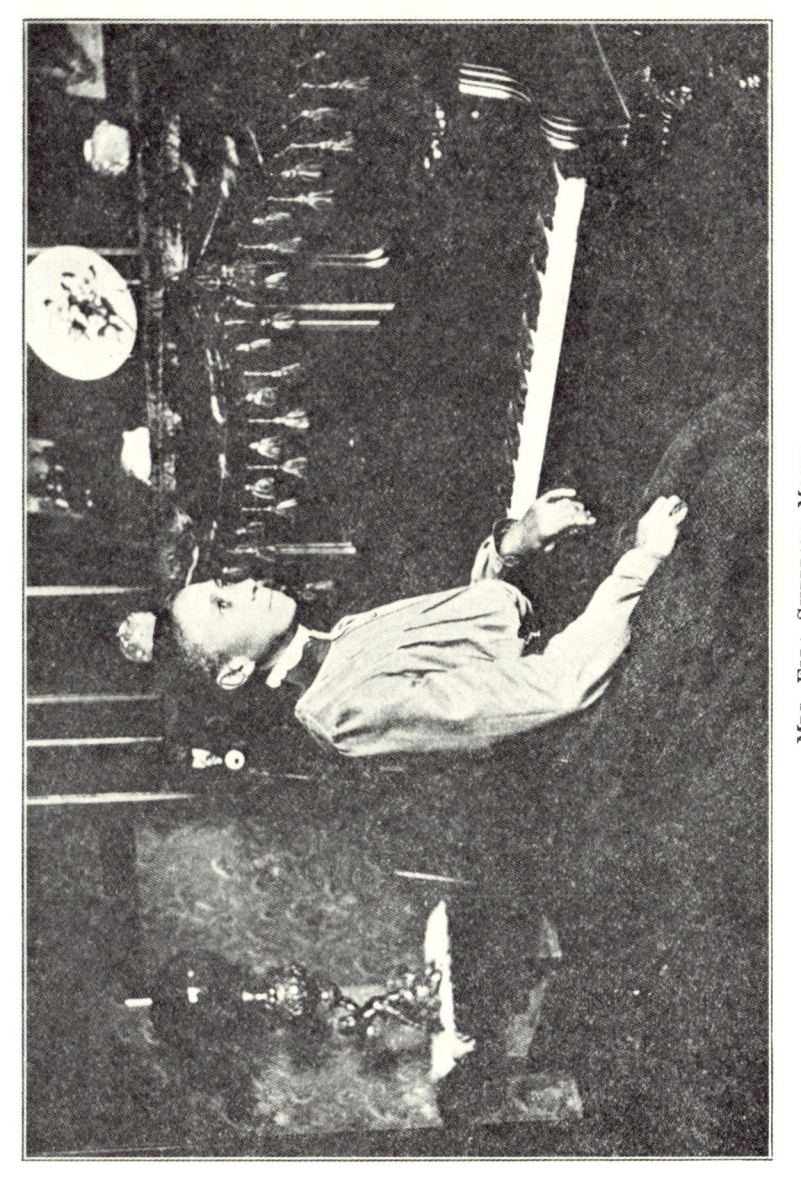

Mrs. Ella Sheppard Moore,

Who, as a babe in arms, was rushed to a watery grave, when her mother was stopped by a fellow slave and was told a great prophecy.

being sung at her bedside, she awoke and make a supreme effort to join in the melody. That baby girl was Ella Sheppard, who afterwards became the pianist of the Original Jubilee Singers. At the annual meeting of the American Missionary Association in Burlington, Vermont, General O. O. Howard was one of the speakers. Before he delivered his address, he requested the Fisk Quartette to sing for him "Swing Low, Sweet Chariot," adding that he felt it would not be long before the chariot would swing low for him. As the quartette sang, the General stood and listened as tears filled his eyes. He then touched all hearts present with the pathos of a stirring address. A few days later, the chariot swung low and bore the General home.

"Most done toilin' here;
Um! Most done toilin' here!"

This song was born since freedom and is one of the very few real folk songs that were produced by freedom. It is really a "new song" of Virginia. It leaped almost wholly from the heart of a good woman who simply wanted something new to sing. She doubtless gave some thought to it and to a certain degree it was "composed, but in spirit and melody it is a true folk song. The good woman who gave me the history of this song, told it in these words: "We simply wanted a new song to sing in church, and we just started to sing this song. Our troubles weighted us down, and, of course, we were thinking of them more than anything else. It came to me this way, 'Um! most done toiling here,' and I sang it; another sister added something else, and it kept on until we had a 'new song.' "

"You may bury me in the East,
You may bury me in the West,
But I'll hear the trumpet sound,
In-a that mornin'."

If there is in all the collections of folk song a pure melody this is it. It is the song of faith. It was born in Georgia, near Atlanta. A slave was sold from his wife and it seemed that he would really die of broken heart, but as he was being led away he said with a wail:

"You may bury me in the East,
You may bury me in the West,
But I'll hear the trumpet sound,
In-a that mornin'."

This song was the favorite of Dr. E. M. Cravath, the first president of Fisk University.

"Great camp meeting";
"Goin' to moan and never tire."

This song was made by a company of slaves who were not allowed to sing or pray in the hearing of their master. And when he died, the old mistress, looking upon them with pity, granted them the privilege of singing and praying in their cabins at night. Then they sang their hymn, shouted for joy, and gave God honor and praise. This song, magnificent in composition, subtle in application, presents an extremely interesting study. It pictures Heaven as a great camp meeting. The Negro's imagination could find no more satisfying analogy. The camp meeting was an occasion of joy, which expressed itself in eating, drinking, singing, praying, shouting, and resting from fields of corn, cotton, and rice, and all the while there was communion with God. Heaven could be no more, except that this meeting went on forever. There they would sing, shout, moan, and never tire. It seems, at first, strange that there should be any moaning in the Negro's Heaven. But this was a paradox. The "moan" was joyful. In the big meetings, there was a certain set of church members set aside to lead in the moaning, a low plaintive fragment of melody, sometimes a hum and sometimes accompanied by words of striking character. This is done to help the preacher as he pours out his sermon, which is generally a vivid description of hell and destruction awaiting the sinner. This moan is the accompaniment to the sermon and the combination has sometimes wonderful effect upon the unconverted. History records that Gaius Gracchus used to deliver his great orations to the Roman people to the accompaniment of a stringed instrument. The most effective Greek oration was that which was most melodious. Melody is always effective, especially that which is spontaneous. No one who ever heard the moan could fail to be deeply impressed. From the rural districts of West Tennessee came the one that follows:

"O Lord, O Lord, O Lord!
Somebody's dying, somebody's dying, somebody's dying
Every day, every day, every day."

The tune is more plaintive than the lay of the whippoorwill or the call of the sorrowing dove. Such is the meaning of "moan and never tire," and it seemed to inspire the preacher with heavenly zeal and celestial vision. It is not likely that this shout sprang complete from the soul of any single creator, as Minerva from the brain of Jupiter. This is unthinkable, for it is too comprehensive, too full of meaning, too purposeful and too finished to be of extemporaneous birth. The beginnings and essentials were doubtless of a moment's inspiration, but most assuredly the song complete is a product of development. This process of evolution is clear. While this song is apparently a picture of Heaven created by the Negro's imagination, it is more than that; it is a consolation to the slaves in their distress and the expression of the firm expectation that freedom was coming.

The song, "Bright Sparkles in the Church Yard," is the incoherent wailing of a delirious soul suffering from the remorse of waywardness. The most authentic and reliable history names a wayward girl as the producer of this song. She has left the paths laid out for her by her sainted mother, and the wild, riotous fires have consumed her life forces and brought her down through sickness, pain, and sorrow to the brink of death. In her delirium she cries out:

"May the Lord, He will be glad of me,
In the Heaven, He'll rejoice."

Her loneliness with the thought that the world cares little or nothing for her, brings her to the last resort. The Lord cares for her, maybe; maybe, He'll be glad to see her, even if the world is cold and cruel. The fireflies flashing in the darkness of the graveyard add to her loneliness in the summer night.

"Bright sparkles in the churchyard,
Give light into the tomb;
Bright summer, spring's over—
Sweet flowers in their bloom."

The springtime of her life has passed into summer, and summer, with its flowers, has withered and gone.

"My mother once, my mother twice, my mother, she'll rejoice,
In the Heaven once, in the Heaven twice, she'll rejoice."

The love of her mother now in Heaven will welcome her from the heartless world. "Mother, rock me in the cradle, all the day," was her longing for the purity of infancy, where there was no blight or stain, when the crooning voice of her mother sang soothing lullabies, sweetly lulling her to a blameless sleep.

> "O mother, don't you love your darling child?
> O rock me in the cradle all the day!"

There would be some consolation in the assurance that mother loved her "darling child," who, though she had left the paths her mother had shown her and begged her to tread, though the stain of impurity was upon her soul, still was her mother's darling child.

> "You may lay me down to sleep, my mother, dear;
> O rock me in the cradle all the day!"

The sleep of her childhood days would free her from care, from stain, from sorrow.

> "Let us cheer the Weary Traveler,
> Let us cheer the Weary Traveler,
> Let us cheer the Weary Traveler,
> Along the lonesome Way."

"Aunt Ailsie" was a slave in Augusta County, Virginia. She was a powerful specimen of womanhood; her face was brown and sweet; her voice was soft and mellow; she was a woman of few words, but capable, and as a servant, invaluable. Her disposition was wholly lovable until she was angered, and then she was a lioness robbed of her cubs. "Aunt Ailsie" had greatly provoked her master, who would have killed her had she not been too valuable. He decided to sell her South. The slave trader bought her, placed her in his "gang" and went to Staunton on the first stage of the journey. They pitched camp on Sunny Hill, on the outskirts of the town. "Uncle Chester Bowling," her brother, heard the news and went out to Sunny Hill, and begged the trader to let him keep his sister in his cabin over night. The trader yielded, and that night the cabin was full of prayers and songs. Her slave friends came in and stayed all night. Not an eyed closed that night. They sang and prayed for help and comfort for "Aunt Ailsie," and when the bright morn of nature broke upon the world, "Aunt Ailsie" turned her way to the slave gang, bound for the South. The weary, heart-bowed slaves, in weird vioce, sang:

> "Let us cheer the Weary Traveler,
> Let us cheer the Weary Traveler,
> Let us cheer the Weary Traveler,
>   Along the lonesome Way."

> "If you meet with trials and troubles on de way—
> Jis' put yo' trus' in Jesus, an' don't forget to pray."

> "Nobody knows the trouble I see, Lord,
> Nobody knows the trouble I see;
> Nobody knows the trouble I see, Lord;
> Nobody knows like Jesus."

"Uncle Anthony" was owned by an Augusta County master, and lived happily with his faithful wife. Their cabin was a realm of melody. It was singing, singing, singing! One day, Heaven sent a child to them, and there was more singing, with a tenderer, more ecstatic note. The glad father worked at odd times upon a rude cradle for his babe, in which she could lie, rock, and go to sleep to the comforting lullabies from the full-hearted mother. At last the cradle was finished, and with an overflowing soul he bore it home. His joy grew with every step; anticipations of opening the door of that cabin, seeing the baby in the cradle, and beholding the smile upon that mother's face made his his heart swell and his breath come short and fast! The cabin was there; that was all! Mother and babe were gone with the trader, somewhere toward the South. The bud of his happiness was dead! He searched the whole creation for his wife and child. The forests, hills, and fields mocked his cries. Days and days he was a madman in his grief. No threats or lashings could quiet him or force him back to his work. His usefulness as a slave was destroyed, and when a man whose heart had been touched and softened by the poor slave's sorrow offered to buy him, his offer was at once accepted. Two thousand dollars he paid, and received his purchase of flesh and blood. The bargain closed, he immediately made out "free papers" for Anthony and told him to go find his wife and child, promising that if he found them, they, too, should be purchased and freed. The last account of him was that he was still pursuing his quest somewhere in North Carolina, with this song upon his lips:

"Nobody knows the trouble I see, Lord,
Nobody knows the trouble I see;
Nobody knows the trouble I see, Lord;
Nobody knows like Jesus."

"Good morning, Everybody!"

The place and time of this song's birth are uncertain, but it is certain that it grew out of the following conditions: The test of "true heart-felt religion" among Negroes is love for everybody and the one way of showing this love is to "speak" to everybody, especially to those with whom one has not been upon agreeable terms. It was the custom of the new convert, or the Christian who "got happy" to run first, if possible, to those who were his enemies, shake hands, embrace, and tell what a "dear loving Saviour" he had found; that his soul was "alive" and that he had nothing against anybody. The never-failing sign of hypocrisy in religion was a refusal to express love for, or to speak to, everybody. The originator of this song was simply meeting the test of "true, heart-felt religion" when he went into the field to work with the salutation, "Good mornin', everybody." It was in this state of happiness that the Negro sang of "heaven an' immortal glory" with all the robes, crowns, slippers, gates, streets, which made Heaven so real to him.

"Go down, Moses—"

"Way down in Egypt land, tell ole Pharaoh
Let my people go."

While this song is a simple chronicle of an event in biblical history, it is just as plainly preaching freedom "in a Bibleistic way." The stanzas are quite numerous, running up to thirty-six in one edition of folk songs, but doubtless many are spurious. The very best explanation of this song is given in Dunbar's "Antebellum Sermon," where an old Negro preacher is interpreting slavery in terms of

Egyptian bondage, every now and then throwing out the hint that freedom was coming to the Negro, too. This song, from certain bits of information gathered from a surprising source, is hoary with age. Either the Negroes got this melody from the Hebrews, or the Hebrews got it from the Negroes. The time was probably the age of the Pharaohs. However, it may be, the Hebrews claim it as one of their folk songs, the subject being "Cain and Abel." The following interesting piece of information was given me by a social worker among the Russian Jews, in Henry Street Settlement, New York City:

"I was holding a Woman's Meeting one evening, and to help things move along, asked the women to sing one of their own songs. To my surprise, one began the tune of 'Go Down, Moses,' and the others followed. I was greatly interested, and asked them what the song was. I was told that it was one of their folk songs, 'Cain and Abel.' Desiring to satisfy mself in this matter, I held another meeting of Hebrew women who were not at the former meeting, and as a part of their exercises I sang, 'Go Down, Moses.' They recognized it as their song, 'Cain and Abel.' Whether of Hebrew or of Negro origin, there seems to be no way of determining, but it bears all the evidences of the Negro music. In plaintiveness, in intervallic changes, in melody, in scale, in rhythm, and in spirit, it has all evidence of Negro origin."

"I'm troubled in mind."

This song was born in a Tennessee plantation and was the burden of an old slave's lamentation, after he had been flogged. So piteously did he sing it that even the overseer was not unmoved. After each whipping he would sit upon an old log, the same one every time, rest his head upon his hand and pour out this wail. After he had wept thus in melody and experienced for a few short moments the inexplicable joy of resentless suffering, he went anew to the humdrum tasks of a slave.

Other songs are just as romantic in their nativity, but the mystery of their birth forbids our telling their stories. Each song is a product of sudden inspiration and subtle evolution with a meaning definite and consoling to the slave. In birth, in development and in the meaning, each song is an inspiring study.

STEAL AWAY TO JESUS

Steal a-way, steal a-way, steal a-way to Je-sus!

Steal a-way, steal a-way home, I ain't got long to stay here!

1. My Lord calls me, He calls me by the thun-der;
2. Green trees are bend-ing, poor sin-ner stands a-tremb-ling;
3. Tomb-stones are burst-ing, poor sin-ner stands a-tremb-ling;
4. My Lord calls me, he calls me by the light-ning;

The trum-pet sounds with-in-a my soul, I ain't got long to stay nere.

CHAPTER VII.

Agencies of Preservation and Development.

"I verily think and am not ashamed to say that, next to Divinity, no art is comparable to music."

NOTWITHSTANDING the facts that forty-five years have elapsed since the Negro Folk Music was first given to the world by the Original Fisk Jubilee Singers, and notwithstanding the first burst of consuming enthusiasm with which it was received has about all passed away, still there is to-day a more serious interest taken in it than ever before.

In the early days it was looked upon as a curiosity in the world of song, beautiful, entertaining but transient, for the world never considered it more than a commodity, through which one or two Negro schools maintained themselves. It was fully expected that when these schools drew in their companies of singers, this music would die. It is probable that it owes its life and much of its currency largely to Hampton Institute, which has been very consistent in collecting and singing it.

Now, at Fisk, Hampton, Tuskegee, and Calhoun earnest and serious efforts are being put forth to collect, sing, study, and develop it. This work on the part of the centers of learning insures a permanency which this music most certainly deserves.

As a result of the efforts of these institutions there are now known to be something over five hundred of these songs, the most beautiful of which are known to the most of us, while others are current only in certain localities.

Doubtless the same methods are used in all the schools engaged in collecting this music. At certain seasons a teacher or student will make excursions into the districts where "big meetings," "camp meetings" or revivals are being held, prepared to reduce to writing the songs he is almost sure to hear. At these special occasions there is a perfect carnival of "Folk Music," for people come from far distant and separated places, bringing different songs, new songs, and varied interpretations of the same songs. Ofttimes there is a real musical contest, which is certain to bring forth a large number of songs. These songs, however, lose much of their character when taken out of their settings. Certain intonations and a certain inexplicable something imparted by those in whose hearts they were born, can never be reproduced otherwise or represented by musical notation. Another method employed is to find out some expert in the knowledge and art of this music, and tactfully request him to sing the songs to be copied. There is in every locality of this kind, one person, or perhaps two, from whom many of these melodies may be obtained. Success in this method is a variable quantity, for sometimes just as soon as it is learned that some teacher or student is present for the purpose of learning these songs, the memory of the singer goes wrong or leaves him, his voice is all out of fix, or his lungs refuse to work and his tongue cleaves to the roof of his mouth. Yes, this or even worse than this is often the case. Under these circumstances it takes all the tact available to get one single note, and most often there is absolute failure. Sometimes, after the first shock has subsided the singer will make copious excuses, close his eyes and begin, and very likely the visitor will get a sufficiency long before the singer decides to cease his song. Sometimes the eyes are not closed, but are viewing the visitor askance, in an effort to detect an indication of insincerity. Another person when asked to sing, will "sail right in" and give what is asked for.

These trips on the hunt for songs are always extremely interesting, and often open up a new world to the searcher. Such rare truths are learned, such uplifting knowledge gained, such beautiful voices, such touching sympathies, such noble hearts, such simple and childlike faith, such attractive and expressive features are met, that the visitor is convinced that the Creator has made a fair and just distribution of his blessings.

Another method is to canvass among the students. As a rule there is always a considerable number of students who come from the localities where this music is current, and who are almost always glad to make any possible contribution in this matter.

The formation of clubs for the study of this music is a most effective method for collecting and preserving it. It both interests and instructs, and is the one place where reproduction is truest to nature; for with such singers as are naturally selected for these clubs, it is possible to make them see and understand the minutest point which makes for perfection.

Forty-five years have naturally made some changes in the renderings of certain songs, not so marked, however, as is sometimes supposed. These changes have come about in different ways. The idea, which is now regnant in singing these songs, that of using harmonies of close chords, was first brought forward by some boys in Livingstone Hall, Fisk University, who were whiling away the time between supper and study hour one spring evening. They were members of no organization whatever, but had good voices. The song they liked and were singing was "Golden Slippers," and they were great in making "snakes," their word for close chords, which were so successfully accomplished and which sounded so rare and acceptable that the idea was adopted at once by the folk song organization at Fisk and has now become a fixed part of the folk music.

In addition to this, there has been a studied endeavor at development which has produced some new harmonies and arrangements much preferable to the old ones. In truth, the general adaptability of this music to a high degree of development is its hope of gaining artistic recognition. It deserves to be put into a finished form; it lends itself admirably to such a purpose; and those who would keep it as it was first reduced to writing, in their mistaken zeal would doom it to stagnation and to the contempt of highly musical people.

Where we find these songs there is no harmony, nothing but melody and words. The harmony is a matter of individual taste. That is why there is a difference in rendering.

Undoubtedly the best results in singing, in point of nuance, are obtained in a musical organization; but for striking down deep into the soul and stimulating every lofty emotion, for arousing men's hearts to action, the singing of these songs by a large congregation is as indescribable as melodious thunder or as the rushing of many waters.

We sometimes hear this lamentation, "It is too bad that the old plantation melodies are dying out." Such laments are felt more keenly and expressed more fully by the Southern white man who was a part of the system of slavery, than by any other class. It is no sickly sentimentality but a deep feeling for a life, the memory of which is dear. For these 'old songs" link the Southern white man to a romantic past. That past was full of poetry, and though often tragic, it was a life of tender and strong relations, when the "black mammies" with their great big hearts and mystic wisdom, loved and reared ten generations of masters. It was a time when the rich plantation rang with the sweetly lonesome melodies of the faithful slave. No mortal could forget those days. Such regrets were much to the point thirty-five years ago before the educated Negroes began to study, understand, and appreciate their old songs, but this danger is now forever past. While, however, we shall always preserve these songs, in their original forms and while we shall always go back to them for inspiration and history "lest we forget," they can never be the "last word" in the development of our music. In other words, they are our starting point, not our goal; the source, not the issue, of our music. The Negro ought never be content with the folk songs as they are, but should work for development, which would bring them into a more exalted life. This is just what is being done by the agencies of preservation and development. Among these agencies, are educational institutions, musical organizations, and individuals. The educational institutions foremost in this work are Fisk Universty, Hampton Institute, Atlanta University, Talladega College, Tuskegee Institute, and Calhoun School. In addition to these there are numerous others, both private and public. Each one of these institutions is carrying on the work of preservation or development or both, in its own way. The character of the work depends almost wholly upon the conditions surrounding them. Fisk first gave them to the world, through that band of Jubilee Singers which left Nashville on October 6, 1871, to raise funds for a starving institution. This day is still celebrated each year, with appropriate ceremonies. These songs are of much traditional value at Fisk, and are inseparably interwoven with the life of the University. Jubilee Hall has been called "frozen music," significant of the fact that it was erected by money earned by the "Original Fisk Jubilee Singers." Fisk has done the most toward development of this music. Several editions of the Folk Songs have been issued, containing "new songs" as they are found. These songs along with the favorite "old songs" have been adorned with new harmonies more in keeping with the idea of development. These harmonies have not all been studied out, as a composer would do, but often they have been written as they have been sung by the students naturally and without instructions. Such method, we think, is more interesting, and since it is more natural, is more nearly correct and certainly most effective. To explain: When the chorus is singing one of these songs, some voice strikes an entirely new and pleasing note in the harmony. This singer is often unconscious of his departure, oftentimes he knows little if anything of the theory of music. Then, again, small groups of students get together to "harmonize" or "chord." Here, too, new and striking combinations of tones are sometimes struck. Again, some of the musical organizations, composed of those who really understand the technique of music, in searching for harmonies, glide into certain resolutions which are entirely new. All of these are immediately written into their appropriate songs and become parts of them. The plan here has been to combine natural, spontaneous melody with natural, spontaneous harmony. The result has been a most natural kind of satisfaction. Of course, in some measure the harmonies have been worked out according to the rules of the theory of harmony.

The most decided effort at development at Fisk was a cantata, "Out of the Depths," which was rendered publicly several times in Nashville. It is still in manuscript. It tells the story of a slave girl who was sold from her parents, to go down South, and describes the scene just before and at the time of parting, the struggle and trials of her life, "The Camp Meeting," the "Big Meeting," the scenes common to slave life, and the coming of freedom. Into this cantata all the best of the folk songs are brought, but some of them are so changed that they seem new. Probably the most effective of all is the "Bright Sparkles in the Church Yard," which is developed into a touching lullaby. "I am Troubled in Mind," "O Wretched Man that I Am," "You May Bury Me in the East," are used effectively as solos. The changes in "Couldn't Hear Nobody Pray" add some strength and power, while the climax is reached in "Free at Last." No claims of especial merit are made for this cantata, but it does show the possibilities in the folk songs for development.

Those who have been at different times head of Fisk University have had some "favorite" among the folk songs.

Dr. Erastus M. Cravath simply loved "You May Bury in the East," and he never let pass an opportunity to have Mrs. Agnes Haynes Work sing that song.

Dr. James G. Merrill enjoyed to the uttermost the "Great Camp Meeting" as the student body would pour it forth in torrents of harmony.

Dr. George A. Gates, on any occasion whatever, would call for "Made My Vow to the Lord," and never failed to evince his pleasure as he listened to it.

Dr. C. W. Morrow always loves and calls his song, "In-a-my Heart." All these have shown a broad-minded interest in the folk music, each in a different and peculiar way, and have closely identified themselves with it.

Dr. Cravath toured Europe with the original company, Dr. Merrill toured America with the third company during the years 1899-1903, and Dr. Gates campaigned with the Fisk Male Quartette, 1909-1910. Dr. Morrow's connection has been mainly confined to University life in its religious aspects. While he was pastor of the University Church he arranged an order of service with a jubilee song immediately following his sermon. This custom is still followed. One of these songs is always sung to clinch the thought of the sermon.

At Hampton, the spirit and attitude are admirable. It is doubtful if at any place this music is more thoroughly appreciated. Through all these years since its founding, Hampton has steadily collected and published these songs in attractive form. Their editions have been more thorough, more painstaking and more important than those of any other school. There has been, however, practically no effort at development, until quite recently. The songs have been written and published in their original forms, just as they came from the people, and the harmonies have been written with no particular significance.

In interpretation, Hampton has always done well. She has stood far forward. This may be due to the fact that Virginia has a most interesting and fine class of Negroes. They are full of folk lore, folk song, and folk spirit. It is fortunate for this institution that Major R. R. Moton stands as the chief exponent of this music. His spirit and understanding are commendable. Doubly fortunate is it that Hampton has secured the services of R. Nathaniel Dett for the head of her music department. His arrangement of the folk song, "Listen to the Lambs," is meritorious and marks the beginning of the period of development in Negro Folk Song in Hampton. It would not be surprising if under his leadership this institution would be the foremost in both preservation and development.

In the work of preservation the Calhoun School has done some notable work. Its edition of these songs is a distinct credit to itself. The singing of this music at this school, in spirit at least, could not be surpassed.

Tuskegee Institute has lately begun to collect and publish these songs, showing marked progress in development. Mrs. Jennie C. Lee has done a good work in this line. Her choruses interpret and render this music with splendid effect and she herself understands it as very few people do. A most interesting work was done by N. Clark Smith, in stamping this music with some distinctive features. Tuskegee has probably the broadest opportunity of any of the schools for this work. It is in a locality wealthy in folk songs and its fifteen hundred students are a fruitful source as well as a fine force for the production of them.

Atlanta University and Talladega College have both contributed to the work of preservation through their attitude and through their different musical organizations.

One of the most interesting points in this matter is that schools all over the country are beginning serious study of this music. Public schools, especially in the South, are beginning to use it; all of which means that the folk song of the American Negro is rising to new life.

Musical organizations that have helped to preserve this music, in one way or another, are numerous, some worthy, some not. Many organizations caught by greed for "easy money" have toured this country, aping and badly imitating the companies who, in the right spirit and from the best motives, have sung these songs. These spurious "Jubilee Singers" have done the world no good; in fact, they have so maltreated and lowered the folk music that it will require much time and effort to raise it again to the respect due it. They have prostituted it to base desire for lucre. Happily, however, some companies separate and apart from any institution, have maintained a high standard in singing this music. The most prominent of those now before the public is the company of "William Singers." It is composed of four male and four female voices, well balanced and well trained. These singers have a high ideal and are a positive force for good.

Among the individuals who are or have been angencies of preservation may be named, George L. White and Professor A. K. Spence, of Fisk University; Miss Mary E. Spence, his daughter; Mrs. Ella Sheppard Moore, of the Original Fisk Jubilee Singers; Fred J. Work, of Kansas City, Missouri; Harry T. Burleigh; Dr. C. J. Ryder; Dr. W. E. B. DuBois; Miss Kitty Cheatham; Dr. Henry E. Krehbiel; Antonin Dvorak; and Samuel Coleridge-Taylor. There are others who are spoken of elsewhere in this book.

Mr. George L. White might well be called the miracle man of Negro Folk Song. It was he who really faced an opposing world in his purpose to send out those first Jubilee Singers, who, through these strange melodies, overcame mountainous prejudice, and won the hearts of the world.

Professor Adam K. Spence always had an intense interest in this music. He was a poet and philosopher and from the very first saw the real worth of these songs. He resurrected them for the religious worship in Fisk University, and it was he alone who taught the later generation of students to love and respect them. Miss Mary E. Spence is of one and the same spirit with her father. She has always been a helpful force in this work.

Mrs. Ella Sheppard Moore might properly be called a "folk song of the American Negro." She has been so closely connected with the presentation of them to the world, so intimately associated with their preservation that it is impossible to think of the one separate and apart from the other.

Frederick J. Work has collected, harmonized, and published more Negro folk songs and probably has a better technical knowledge of this music than any other individual. The work of that cantata, "Out of the Depths," mentioned before, is largely his original work. He has contributed some helpful articles upon the subject to different journals and has edited a book of songs for a prominent publishing company.

Harry T. Burleigh is doubtless the foremost musician of our race, and has applied his splendid powers to the development of our music. His voice and his mind make an admirable combination for the work. He has transcribed and harmonized several of the best known of these songs which are being used in large choruses. His accurate and sympathetic interpretations are among the brightest accomplishments in this field of endeavor.

Miss Kitty Cheatham, born in the South of parents who owned slaves, has had fine environments and opportunity for the study and understanding of the slave music. It was her family that owned Ella Sheppard. She is one of the few outside of the Negro race who have an adequate understanding and appreciation of this music. She approaches it with the right spirit and proper motive. Her renderings are sympathetic and characteristic. Her religious nature helps her to a serious study of these songs. In addition to this, her life among those who produced them made it most natural for her to get into the spirit of the Negro.

Dr. C. J. Ryder was connected with the campaign of the original band of singers and has had good opportunity to see the effect of these songs upon people's hearts. His long service with the American Missionary Association has kept him in close touch with the Negroes and their songs. He has, for a long time, studied the songs and has delivered some interesting lectures upon them. His study has been from the viewpoint of religion.

Dr. W. E. B. DuBois has devoted one chapter in his book, "Souls of Black Folk," to the songs of his fathers. His viewpoint is that of the philosopher who sees in these songs the life of a people, the possibilities of the future written in the past, the story of admirable strength developed through burden bearing, and purification by fire. This one chapter is a weighty contribution to the preservation and perpetuation of these songs. "Ever since I was a child," says he, "these songs stirred me strangely. They came out of the South unknown to me; one by one, and at once, I knew them as of me and of mine."

Dr. Henry E. Kriehbiel has for more than a quarter of a century been a faithful student of the Negro Folk Song. He has analyzed, described and harmonized many specimens. He has lectured and written upon the subject and has published a book, "Afro-American Folk Songs." His viewpoint is that of the musician. He has a broad knowledge of the music and the work he has done is important and efficient.

Dr. Antonin Dvorak made in some ways the most effective pronouncement ever made regarding this music. When he announced that the only original music America could claim was the music of the Negro, he mildly startled the United States of America. There is no doubt that he successfully defended his position, for the majority of the most important composers in this country are with him. He suggested that this music would lend itself to higher development, and that it would be a basis for a national music.

Acting upon his own suggestion, Dvorak composed the symphony, "From the New World," in which he endeavored with eminent success, to preserve the characteristic feature of the Negro music. Others have followed his example; among whom are Chadwick, Schoenberg, and Kroeger.

Samuel Coleridge-Taylor has transcribed several of the folk songs, and, in fact, has transformed them into classics. It is true that they do not throb with American life, but they throb with human feeling. They were born to immortal life. His "Sometimes I Feel Like a Motherless Child" and "Deep River" are the most successful of his transcriptions, and point the way toward the future where lives the dream and hope of the Negro race, which, too, was seen by Dvorak.

No, these songs cannot die. They are eternal.

WERE YOU THERE?

1. Were you there when they cru - ci - fied my Lord? (were you there?)
2. Were you there when they nailed Him to the tree? (to the tree?)
3. Were you there when they pierced Him in the side? (in the side?)
4. Were you there when the sun re - fused to shine? (were you there?)
5. Were you there when they laid Him in the tomb? (in the tomb?)

Were you there when they cru - ci - fied my Lord? Oh!............
Were you there when they nailed Him to the tree? Oh!............
Were you there when they pierced Him in the side? Oh!............
Were you there when the sun re - fused to shine? Oh!............
Were you there when they laid Him in the tomb? Oh!............

Some- times it caus - es me to trem - ble, trem - ble,
Some- times it caus - es me to trem - ble, trem - ble,
Some- times it caus - es me to trem - ble, trem - ble,
Some- times it caus - es me to trem - ble, trem - ble,
Some- times it caus - es me to trem - ble, trem - ble,

trem - ble, Were you there when they cru - ci - fied my Lord?
trem - ble, Were you there when they nailed Him to the tree?
trem - ble, Were you there when they pierced Him in the side?
trem - ble, Were you there when the sun re - fused to shine?
trem - ble, Were you there when they laid Him in the tomb?

CHAPTER VIII.

THE TOUR OF THE ORIGINAL JUBILEE SINGERS.

> *"For Orpheus' lute was strung with poet's sinews,*
> *Whose golden touch could soften steel and stones;*
> *Make tigers tame, and huge leviathans*
> *Forsake unsounded deeps to dance on sands."*

THESE songs were never intended for the world at large. On the contrary, they were lines of communication between the slaves and God, and between the slave and slave. The slave never dreamed that the world cared for his song, nor did he dream that his song had a message for the world. So he sang in the field, in the cabin, and in the meeting house, to lighten his burden, to comfort his brother, and to entreat his God. All these were the personal concern of the slave, and not in the least the concern of the world. The world was big, cold, and awful, and not only cared not for his song, but had not one spark of real human interest in him, the maker and singer of his song. No! not the world! But the secret place, the lonesome valley, the purple dawn, solitudes all wet with dews, and God away off in the listening Heavens, they would hear his songs. They did hear. But lo! this humble singer knew not how near to pure glory he was, nor did he know into what effective means of salvation he had been fashioned. This strange new song fairly burst upon the world; burst from unwilling hearts upon unwilling hearts.

A man of faith and vision came from New York State to work among the freedmen, in a school founded in the city of Nashville by the American Missionary Association. This school had been given the name of Fisk. It was to offer the opportunity for higher education to those who for two and a half hundred years had been slaves, and whose ancestors for untold centuries had lived in the wilds of Africa. After the first bloom of success had faded from this novel "experiment," and men began to proclaim, "It is not worth while," then strong men began to grow faint and their faith weakened, their hopes faded and the Fisk School was given up to die. "Man's ex-

The Original Jubilee Singers.

tremity is God's opportunity," is an old proverb and it proved true here. The God who loves and honors faith has, in every crisis, a faithful servant. George L. White had the faith that moves mountains. He had heard the black boys and girls singing their peculiar songs. He was a musician. He felt a moving of his emotion as those weird melodies struck his soul; and, as they touched him, they would touch the world, for the world was himself multiplied over and over again. So these songs must be sung abroad, and men's hearts, touched and softened, would respond with interest. This accomplished, Fisk School would be saved. But in the hearts of those black boys and girls there was the echoing of that thought, "The world cares not for our song." So it was with great difficulty that Mr. White could persuade his scholars to sing their songs in concert. Finally, through tact, patience, and the faith they had in him, he was successful. So he organized his choir and began his training. Even then it was only sometimes that they would sing their own songs. They preferred the white man's music. It soon became known that Mr. White was preparing to lead a troup of his singers into the world that the world might hear their songs. Immediately a mighty protest burst from the mothers and fathers, for to them these songs were sacred, their message-bearers from heart to heart, from here to Heaven. They were to be sung in the dewy dawn down in the valley, in the solitude, and to the far-off listening Heaven. In their hearts there echoed and re-echoed, "The world is not worthy of them."

Mr. White's vision, however, would not leave him, truly it haunted him. He saw Henry Ward Beecher standing up before his great congregation commending these singers and their songs to the sympathies of those who listened in tears. He saw philanthropy pour out its money with its tears; he saw the scoffers bow their heads and raise them up again with fairest words of praise. He saw the blue expanse of the broad Atlantic beyond which England's sorrowing queen was speaking words of gratitude for the comfort these singers and their songs had brought her; he saw the palace in Pottsdam and the royal family listening with evident approval to these strange, new songs; he saw the nobles bringing gifts and the peasants and those in prison shedding tears and heaving sighs, more precious than frankincense and myrrh. He saw Fisk rise in the newness and strength of life. He saw his faith justified. All this he saw in the far-off distance. That is the way of faith. Had he been timid and fearful; had he lacked a breadth of vision; had he looked closely and narrowly, he would have seen cold, staring faces, faces sneering and faces hostile. He would have seen cold, snowy nights, and black boys and girls shivering with him, as they trudged from inn to inn, hotel to hotel, boarding house to boarding house, to find shelter from the bitter cold; he would have seen empty halls in which they sang, and himself selling his wife's jewelry, her wedding presents and his own personal belongings, with which to pay bills; he would have seen himself standing up humbly before scant audiences begging some man to give him enough money to pay railroad fare to the next engagement. He would have seen Metropolitan newspapers heartlessly cartooning his singers, ridiculing them and hurling at them "Nigger Minstrels."

He might have seen all this, but he did not. It was a mercy, for such a vision might have done damage even to his faith and courage. So, inspired by his own vision, tactfully, but directly in the face of protests, Mr. White continued in his course. At designated intervals he would gather his choir into a room, close the door and the windows as closely as advisable, and rehearse in pianissimo tones, the song of the cabin and of the field. The training of this company was a work of patience. Many were the devices and methods to teach them the proper tone production. The smoothing down of their voices was an accomplishment which came after long and hard labor. It was easy to approach this music, and assume an attitude neither reverential nor serious, and in all probability had this course been followed the initiation of the company into the world of entertainment would have been smoother, but they could never have attained to that grand success which they did work out. Finally, understanding this, Mr. White taught them to enter into the spirit and feeling of their fathers when they sang their fathers' songs.

There was another who saw a vision. It was Ella Sheppard. She saw her mother with her babe in her arms, rushing madly to leap over the bluffs of the Cumberland down into the deep waters; she saw the dear old Aunt Jane, as she laid her restraining hand upon the arm of the frenzied mother, while in kindly voice she said, "Don't you do it, honey; God's got a great work for this child to do. She's goin' to stand before kings and queens of this earth. Don't you do it, honey." Oh, the joys that filled her soul as she anticipated the fulfillment of this prophecy!

It was the sixth day of October in the year of our Lord, one thousand eight hundred and seventy-one, when George L. White started out from Fisk School with his eleven students to raise money, that Fisk might live. Professor Adam K. Spence, who was principal of the school, gave Mr. White all the money in his possession save one dollar, which he held back, that the treasury might not be empty. While friends and parents wept, waved, and feared, the train puffed out of the station. All sorts of difficulties, obstacles, oppositions, and failures faced them until through wonderful persistence they arrived at Oberlin, Ohio. Here the National Council of Congregational Churches was in session. After repeated efforts, Mr. White gained permission for his singers to render one song. Many of the members of the Council objected vigorously to having the important business of the session interrupted by such songs and such singers. During the time of the session the weather had been dark and cloudy. The sun had not shown one moment, it had not cast one ray upon the village. The singers went into the gallery of the church, unobserved by all save the moderator and a few who were on the rostrum. At a lull in the proceeding, there floated sweetly to the ears of the audience the measures of "Steal Away to Jesus." Suddenly the sun broke through the clouds, shone through windows upon the singers, and verily they were a heavenly choir. For a time the Council forgot its business and called for more and more. It was at this point that Henry Ward Beecher almost demanded of Mr. White that he cancel all engagements and come straight to his church in Brooklyn. They did not cancel all their engagements, but they went to New York as soon as possible. They were cared for by the officers of the American Missionary Association.

Mr. Beecher arranged to have them in his prayer meeting and to introduce them to New York and New England. He carried out his plan admirably. In his own prayer meeting he introduced them in fitting words, telling their mission. After they had sung several of their melodies to the evident enjoyment of the large audience, he arose and said, "I'm going to do what I want every person in this house to do." With these words he turned his pockets inside out and put into the offering plate all the money he had. Others followed, and when the offering was counted it was $1,300.00. The newspapers of New York had full account the next morning, some approving and some ridiculing.

When the Metropolitan newspapers called the company "Nigger Minstrels," Mr. White was face to face with a situation as serious as it was awkward. His company had no appropriate name, and the odium of the title attributed by the New York newspapers pained him intensely. If they were to be known as "Nigger Minstrels," they could never realize his vision; they were both handicapped and checkmated, and their career was dead. One whole night he spent in prayer, and his little band of pupils have borne witness that the next morning his face shone as if, like Moses, he had spoken with God "face to face, as a man speaketh unto his friend." The suggestiveness of the Hebrew Jubilee had been borne in upon his mind, and with the joy of a deep conviction he exclaimed, "Children, you are the Jubilee Singers."

From 1871 to 1878 that company enjoyed one continuous ovation. New England crowded her largest buildings and paid liberally to hear them sing. Mr. White began to send back to Professor Spence hundreds of dollars to add to that one lonely dollar held back to keep from having an empty treasury.

After a most astounding and unexpected success in this country plans were made for touring England. They sang their way into the good graces of the whole of Great Britain from the queen down to the peasant. The queen, the Duke of Argyle, Lord Shaftesbury and Mr. Gladstone did them especial honor, and their concerts were very largely attended. They were the sensation of the kingdom. Not simply because they were strange and novel, but because their singing and their music made a deep impression upon the hearts of all who heard them. Mr. Gladstone gave absorbing attention as they sang for him, and his spontaneous comment was, "Isn't it wonderful!" The good Queen Victoria wept, and declared that she had received no such comfort as this, from any other source, since the death of her consort. Dwight L. Moody, who was conducting evangelistic services in London at the time, used them whenever he could get them, and hundreds were converted to the better life. The English people paid large sums to hear them sing and loaded them down with gifts and gratitude.

The English *Independent*, April 2, 1874, in an article, "Jubilee singers at Edetan Hall," states:

"Lord Shaftesbury, at the close, said they had received the singers with the deepest sympathy and now rejoiced at the greatness of their success. He eulogized the self-denial and patriotism of "these pious young people" for their exertions to exalt their race, and said that the affection and respect of the English people would follow them wherever they went. After a few words addressed to the singers by his lordship, the doxology was sung by the entire assembly, and Lord Shaftesbury, amid the cheers of the audience, shook hands with each of the singers as they quitted the platform."

They spent eight months in Germany with experiences similar to those they had in England. They were welcomed, heard, and entertained by royalty, nobility, and peasant. They sang, by special engagements, before the leading critics of Germany.

Perhaps the final word of criticism from Germany was this: "They disarm the critic." The visits to Great Britain and to Germany were the most notable of their campaigns. Their fame spread rapidly and "gained strength by going," until their songs resounded round the world. After seven years of such campaigning these humble singers returned to Fisk and laid at her feet $150,000 and many rich gifts. Jubilee Hall, a monument to their sacrifice, stands on the identical spot upon which was once a slave pen. There it stands, lifting up its grateful head to God and His Heaven.

The noble altruism of these singers was ever manifest in their work. Through suffering, they sang to the world strange songs from their bruised hearts. In need of comfort, they comforted the sorrowing. Their courage, their faith, their love for Fisk brought to them the honor of being the first to sing these songs to the world. October 6, 1871, was a great day for Fisk, for it was the day when was made the sacrifice which gave her salvation. But the divinest element of this sacrifice was that not one of that band of singers ever enjoyed the blessing which Fisk has bestowed upon so many. Not one returned to finish his Christian education.

The original company consisted of Ella Sheppard, Jennie Jackson, Maggie Porter, Minnie Tate, Mary Eliza Walker, Thomas Rutling, Benjamin M. Holmes, Green Evans, and Isaac Dickinson. As time passed, there were changes in the personnel. During this seven years, at one time or another, Hinton Alexander, Fred Louden, Mabel Lewis, Georgia Gordon, and America Robinson, were members of the Fisk Company.

A Harwick paper of January 9, 1874, makes the following comment:

"In personal appearance they are far from unprepossessing, three of the young ladies being both handsome and pretty, and their complexion present every variety of the 'colored' from deep black to almost white. Their service of song, regarded as a musical performance is chiefly remarkable for its novelty. The melodies and choruses are of the simplest possible construction, but one or two of them were very picturesque and the harmony exquisite, if not perfect. They have been very highly spoken of by Mr. Gladstone, Mr. Bright, and by the Metropolitan and provincial press."

Fisk has sent out other companies at different times, since the original company made its memorable campaign.

In 1890-1891 a company composed of Misses Linalina Haynes, Alice Vassar, Fanny Snow, Marie Antoniette Crump, and Messrs. John W. Halloway, Paul LaCour and Thos. W. Talley toured the North and East in the interest of the Theological Building.

In 1899 another troup left the University in the general interest of the institution. It was composed of Misses Mabel L. Grant, Ida M. Napier, Lenetta V. Hayes, Edith Bowman, Mrs. Agnes H. Work, and Messrs. S. S. Caruthers, A. E. Greenlow, G. E. Martin, and J. W. Work, the director. This company, with some changes, remained in the field for four years. During these four years Misses Jeanette Washington, Katherine Rainey, Florence Pamplin, Marie Antoniette Crump, Henrietta H. Crawley, Elnora J. Work; Messrs. J. A. Myers, Frederick J. Work, and N. W. Ryder at one time or another were members of this company.

In 1909-1910 the University was represented by a male quartette, the members of which were J. A. Myers, Alfred G. King, N. W. Ryder, and J. W. Work. This quartette was engaged by the Victor Talking Machine Company to make twenty records of folk songs. Of this quartette, Dr. H. E. Krehbiel wrote in the New York *Tribune:*

"A concert goer might live a lifetime and never hear such beautiful homogeneity of tone as that which they produce, nor such euphony, perfection of nuance and precision. Save for its vital human quality, which lifts it above all mechanical products, their harmony sounds like that of a well-attuned organ. A quartette of instinctively excellent artists are these Fisk Singers."

The quality of all the singing at Fisk University since the time of the Original Company has been largely wrought out and maintained through the efficient work of Miss Jennie A. Robinson, who

THE TOUR OF THE ORIGINAL JUBILEE SINGERS. 109

for years has been the teacher of voice culture and the principal of the Music Department. All the singers have been under her personal charge and their ability to sing has resulted in great measure from her teaching. There is always some musical organization in training at Fisk, ever ready to serve the institution in this capacity. Her sons and daughters, loving their fathers' songs, are ever ready with hearts and voices attuned in spirit and understanding to their sacred meaning—to sing, whenever and wherever a heart needs the comfort of a song.

I'm Going to Do All I Can.

Andante.

1. I'm a-going to do all I can for my Lord, I'm a-going to do all I can for my Lord, I'm a-going to do all I can, Till I can't do no more; I'm a-going to do all I can for my Lord.
2. I'm a-going to pray all I can for my Lord, I'm a-going to pray all I can for my Lord, I'm a-going to pray all I can, Till I can't pray no more; I'm a-going to pray all I can for my Lord.
3. I'm a-going to sing all I can for my Lord, I'm a-going to sing all I can for my Lord, I'm a-going to sing all I can, Till I can't sing no more; I'm a-going to sing all I can for my Lord.
4. I'm a-going to mourn all I can for my Lord, I'm a-going to mourn all I can for my Lord, I'm a-going to mourn all I can, Till I can't mourn no more; I'm a-going to mourn all I can for my Lord.
5. I'm a-going to love all I can for my Lord, I'm a-going to love all I can for my Lord, I'm a-going to love all I can, Till I can't love no more; I'm a-going to love all I can for my Lord.

CHAPTER IX.

What the Negro's Music Means to Him.

"The human soul and music are alone eternal."

IN the Negro's own mind his music has held, and still holds, positions of variable importance. In the darkness of bondage, it was his light; in the morn of his freedom, it was his darkness; but as the day advances, and he is being gradually lifted up into a higher life, it is becoming not only his proud heritage, but a support, and powerful inspiration. The songs of the slave were his sweet consolation and his messages to Heaven, bearing sorrow, pain, joy, prayer, and adoration. Undisturbed and unafraid, he could always unburden his heart in these simple songs pregnant with faith, hope, and love. The man, though a slave, produced the song, and the song, in turn, produced a better man. The slave is perennially praised for his perfect devotion. Some attribute it to one cause, some to another. Some even go so far as to attribute it to the influence of the system of slavery, but more than any other cause, the retroactive power of his own music influenced this character of the slave. What else could he be who had such ideals ever before him? How could a man be base who looked ever to the hills? Could a man cherish the idea of rapine whose soul was ever singing these songs of love, patience and God? Neither African heathenism nor American slavery could wholly extinguish that spark of idealism, set aglow by his Creator. This idealism, expressed in terms so beautiful and strong grew in power, and the possessor found himself irresistibly drawn and willingly striving to attain unto it. The creator of these songs had now become the creature of his own creation.

Naturally enough, when the Negro found himself free, he literally put his past behind him. It was his determination that as far as within him lay, not one single reminder of that black past should mar his future. So away went all these reminders into the "abyss of oblivion."

His music was one of these reminders and as sweet as it was to him, as much as it had helped him, it, too, must go, for it was a reminder of the awful night of bondage. It is nothing that newly emancipated slaves sent out by schools like Fisk and Hampton, gained friends and large sums of money by singing these slave songs. That Fisk University can truthfully be said in large part to be a product of these plantation melodies, is nothing against the fact that just after emancipation the Negro refused to sing his own music in public, especially in the schools.

When the Original Fisk Singers started out to earn money for their struggling school, they did not sing their own, but the current music of the day. It was not until they saw that they were doomed to failure that they began to use the plantation melodies, the effectiveness of which was discovered by what was apparently a mere chance. After one crushingly unsuccessful concert, the announcement was made that if any cared to remain for a while after the conclusion of the program, the company would sing a few of their own folk songs. Those who remained showed so plainly their perfect delight, that the singers themselves were astonished. People then began to talk about this new music, not knowing just what to believe about it. It was something similar to curiosity but, in fact, more than that which seized upon the people. The music made men rejoice, it made them weep, it made them ashamed, it made them better. They loved to hear it. All this was positive. The singing of these songs brought ovation after ovation. Though it was a sacrifice of a just pride to sing these songs, the sacrifice, when made, brought a new day, and a new blessing. It introduced the Negro to himself! The Negro is not so different from other men in his thought as he is in his feelings. In thought, he is generic; in feeling, more specific. His feelings are broader and deeper than those of other men and they have more directive influence and power over him than other men's feelings have upon them. This spirituality is the source of his consuming enthusiasm, which has carried him over so many obstacles, to the accomplishment of the all but miraculous. The fact, however, that this feeling is so evident in all his life, work, play, and religion, has led many to conclude that as he abounds in emotion he is lacking in intellect. It is almost unnecessary to state that this inference is a non-sequitur. Like other men, the Negro is affected by his environment, only more deeply affected. He suffers more, he enjoys more. This is one reason why he seems an imitator; this is the reason why he can so easily adapt himself to his surroundings and assume cordial relations with the different phases of life. It is largely on account of this "emotional nature," which so many condemn, that he is monopolizing in different ways so much of the world's attention. Consequently, when we begin to describe the attitude of the Negro toward his own folk song, accuracy demands that we take into consideration time, place, and condition.

Following this course, we shall classify the Negro as follows: (1) Our fathers who came out of bondage. (2a) Those of the first generation of freedom, who grew up in illiberal and intolerant localities. (2b) Those who grew up in localities where the relations between the races were more amicable. (3) The educators; (a) teachers, (b) clergymen, (c) musicians, and (d) authors. (4) The second generation of freedom; (a) those who have lived in the North, (b) those who have lived in the South.

To our fathers who came out of bondage and who are still with us, these songs are prayers, praises, and sermons. They sang them at work; in leisure moments; they crooned them to their babes in their cradles; to their wayward children; they sang them to their sick, wracked with pain on beds of affliction; they sang them over their dead. Blessings, warnings, benedictions, and the very heart beats of life were all expressed to our fathers by their songs. To them there is not one insignificant pause, cadence, inflexion, or expression anywhere in all these countless songs; but every note, every word, every sentiment, is of tremendous import. Yes, those who lived in bondage with these songs, the offspring of their souls still love them as their comforters.

To those of the first generation, who grew up in localities illiberal and intolerant, these songs are generally objects of indifference or aversion. To them slavery is more indefensible than it was to their fathers, and present-day ill-treatment adds to their indignation. Then, too, these songs always remind them of slavery and all slavery meant to their fathers; therefore, the logical sequence is that they either pass them by with "silent contempt," or they regard them with positive apathy. They take neither time nor pains to understand, or if they do this, it is only to condemn. They find all kinds of fault with them, make all kinds of odious comparisons, and "laugh them to scorn." As it is true that mankind will find fault with, criticize, and pick flaws in anything for which he may have conceived a dislike, so it is true that mankind will seek something to praise in anything for which he may have conceived a liking.

As a boy, I was very hard on shoes. My poor father was put to it to keep my feet off the ground. Thinking it was an economy, he always paid a good price for my shoes. When I literally kicked out, burnt out, and ran through those, he decided that he would make a change, and I heard him say to my mother that he was going to buy me brogans. Now, I did not know what brogans were, never heard of them before, but I decided that I did not like these brogans anyway, because there seemed to be in them some reprimand for me. No, I never would like them. In due time, however, my father brought me home a pair of soft calf skin, front-laced shoes with brass tips, no cap, but plain toe. I immediately began to express to the family my dislike for front laces, brass tips, and plain toes; then, too, they did not feel good on my feet, and as I walked around the room there was a positive limp in my gait, because I was sure that that shoe hurt my foot, or would hurt it tomorrow. The only good I could see in that shoe was that it could be cut up into "dandy top-strings" because the leather was so smooth. No persuasions, threats, promises, or the process that generally follows, could make me treat that shoe with friendliness or even common decency. They lived and died the objects of my utter contempt.

Some time after that I took it into by head that high-top boots were good and proper things for a boy to have. So I begged for boots. I dearly loved boots, though I had never had any. My father bought the boots. High tops, brass tips, plain toes, rough leather; I never saw anything prettier. I went into ecstacies over those brass tips, that plain toe, no caps to hurt my feet,—those old caps always did hurt,—then that pretty fuzzy leather! It was rough, too, and would last a long time. I put on my boots, partially and painfully, and walked all over the house to show that they fit all right. If they did hurt a little, they would be all right tomorrow. In agony at my heels, I kept those boots because they were just what I wanted, and while I had them I was going to hold fast to them. No exchanging them for larger ones, they might not come back, and I loved them so. I did not wear those boots out, it was rather the other way. That was many years ago, but I remember them yet, as if they were mine but yesterday. They lived and died the objects of my tenderest affections. My little experience of brogans and boots is enacted by mankind every day. There is not one good point in anything which we do not fancy, nothing undesirable in anything we choose to like.

It is sometimes the case that, by tact and persistence this unfriendly class is brought into a friendly attitude toward this music. There was noteworthy and interesting proof of this at Fisk University. It is clearly paradoxical that for many years it was impossible to induce the students of Fisk to sing these songs, even after that famous first company had sung this institution into new life. For years one would be as likely to hear Negro Folk Songs in St. Peter's at Rome as in Fisk University. But Fisk had no ordinary president. Erastus Milo Cravath was a man of big faith, broad vision, great wisdom and heroic courage, and he knew as well as any living man along what lines the education of the Negro youth should be wrought out. He recognized the importance of the Negro music in the development of the race, and consequently worked to have it incorporated into the life of Fisk. He had a discriminating understanding of this music. He was not a musician, but a philosopher who loved music. To him it was history and prophecy. He was thoroughly convinced that no system of education for the Negro race was complete without his music. His big faith was expressed in the Song of Faith:

> "You may bury me in the East,
> You may bury me in the West,
> But I'll hear the trumpet sound,
> In that morning."

Dr. Cravath had a fine helper in Professor Adam K. Spence, who led the music in chapel, and who was largely responsible for the salvation of the Negro music. When Professor Spence would rise in chapel services and "start" one of these songs, requesting the students to "join in," they would "join in" with a chorus of cold silence. They knew enough to comprehend slavery dialect and bad grammar, and they would have none of either. Elijah, Messiah, and Creation were different and meant better things than the times and conditions represented by these songs. But Professor Spence would analyze and explain individual songs and show their beauty. This he did day in and day out, illustrating with his own sweet voice and sweeter soul the virtues expressed by the music, until he finally led them to an understanding; and now, at all religious services, these

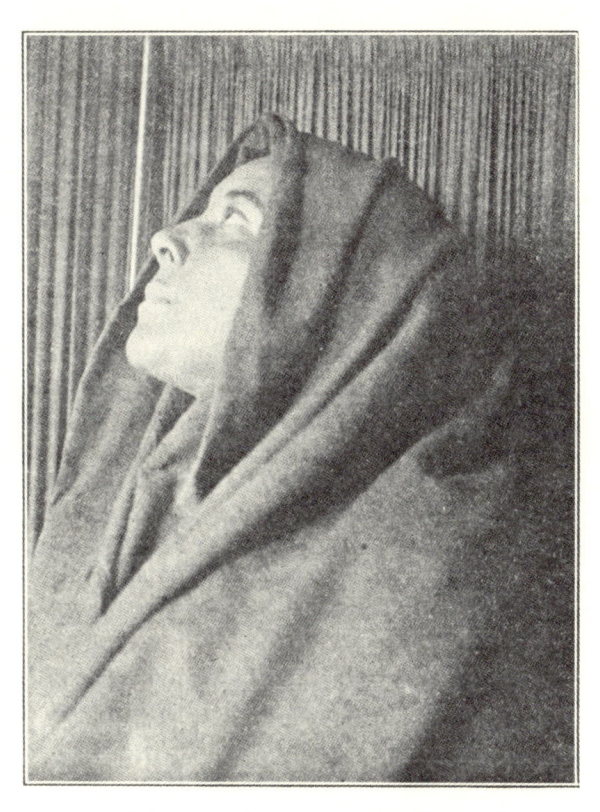

"You may bury me in the East,
You may bury me in the West,
But I'll hear the trumpet soun'
In-a-that mawnin'."

songs are sung in melody abundant and divine. So important a place has this music assumed in the worship and in the life of Fisk that both teachers and students feel that something is lacking, and that there is a distinct loss, if these songs are not sung. These conditions are practically the same in a majority of the southern schools. This growing interest in his own music, the solitary connecting link between the lack of race respect and confidence, and the possibility of race consciousness, is a harbinger of the New Day of Hope.

To us who have been reared in surroundings more pleasant, much of the bitterness of slavery has passed away. In the consideration and kindness of the present, the past is almost forgotten. So to this class, this folk music has a somewhat different meaning. Not consumed by fires of bitter animosity, nor fanned by winds of antipathy, we see every good point of this music. Though we could not forget that it was born in slavery, to us it is beautiful. It does not express itself in the purity of the king's English, but, oh! the crooning sweetness of the dialect! It does not employ the smoothed, well-balanced sentences of the classics, but, oh! the directness, the pithiness, the strength! Its melody does not flow in channels laid out by the great musicians, but, what is more to be praised, its melody is all its own. It is original in its beauty. In its entirety it does not touch with satisfaction the intellects of the standard composers, but it most assuredly touches the heart of all mankind. It may be our fathers' history of their enslaved past, but it is also projecting itself into a future full of bright promise, for he needs not to be called a prophet who predicts that out of our fathers' song there will be evolved a greater song, sublime and glorious. Its coming is foretold by the *forerunners,* Nathaniel Dett, Frederick J. Work, Harry T. Burleigh, Coleridge-Taylor, Henry E. Krehbiel, and Anton Dvorak.

Further, these songs are to us a storehouse of comfort. How can we ever forget those by-gone days when our mothers sang them to us as our lullabies? "This old-time religion, makes me love everybody." Think of the great blessing of being sung to sleep by such a lullaby—"Makes Me Love Everybody!" Think of the great favor of being reared in the atmosphere of "Lord, I Want to be Like Jesus!" In times of sorrow, we have heard our mothers sing "Keep Me from Sinking Down," and often, oh! so often, "March on and You Shall Gain the Victory," has rung with such meaning through the humble home. Can you blame us for loving these songs which have so much inspired us to be and to do?

The study of the attitude of the educators in regard to this music is more interesting than that of any other class. For convenience we have sub-divided this class into (a) teachers, (b) clergymen, (c) musician, (d) authors. While there is generally a favorable attitude among these groups, each group is influenced by their viewpoint, which is determined by their calling. The teachers regard this music as a desirable possession, which is worth study and understanding. They have a feeling of ownership of something original; and if teachers admire any one quality in the course of education, it is originality. They find that this music grips the hearts of the scholars and awakens interest. Teachers always welcome interest in pupils. They find in this music a refreshing departure from the routine of the class room, giving variety to the work. Then there is around this folk song an atmosphere invigorating and inspiring. All this is of practical help to the teacher. Subjectively, the teacher is the better for an understanding of this music, for which his intelligence fits. Not only does he experience intellectual, but spiritual enjoyment as well.

The clergymen's regard is determined almost wholly by the religious power of this music. The wise preacher who really understands his people and the preacher who helps them most, knows that he must take into consideration and give due reverence to the Negro's emotional nature, the whole world to the contrary notwithstanding. Of course, this can be overdone and it often is, but on the other hand many Negro preachers fail because they go too far the other way. They long for the reputation, "intellectual", and discountenance and discourage any manifestations of "feeling." But the arousing of a feeling for the right, is a very nearly sure way of having right done. I am certain that this is psychological heresy, but experience has proved and will continue to prove that the Negro's soul obeys some such law. And the truth is, the souls of some others work the same way. Most men know the right, but it is where they have an enthusiasm for the right, that they will do right. To the preacher these songs of the Negro are powers for arousing "feelings for the right." It is hardly believable that any man could remain the same and unaffected, after singing in the spirit, "Lord, I Want to be Like Jesus," or "Were You There When They Crucified My Lord?" So it seems plain, that the preacher who uses this music to add momentum to the gospel, is wise.

To the musician, these songs furnish both a keen intellectual and a deep emotional enjoyment. He sees their idiomatic features, their characteristic originalities, their smooth exquisite melodies, their thematic values, and their possibilities. He enjoys the wonder of it, that untutored slaves could produce such music, that they could give forth such rhythm, such well balanced periods, such lofty sentiments. He loves to take these old songs and build them into something new without destroying their individuality. He loves to select from them his themes, to be adorned in classic vestments. He loves to build harmonies congenial to their characteristics. He loves to feel that he is working with something original, separate and apart, all his own; he loves to contemplate the future life of this music, which he believes will be a glorious transformation.

The author generally regards this music from an historical and psychological viewpoint. To him it is a reliable account of our people's past. It tells of their suffering and how they bore them, of their joys and how they expressed them, of their lives and how they lived them, how deep and dark were the depths into which they sank, what obstacles they had to surmount. It describes the very tissue of their souls. In short, it tells the stuff of which the Negro is made. With this as a source of facts and inspiration, the author is conscious of a power enabling him to present effectively the cause of his people before the bar of humanity.

Those of the second generation of freedom who have lived in the North, have been more positively and deeply affected in their regard for their racial possessions and characteristics than any other class. They have come nearer experiencing civic and political freedom than their brothers in the South, and have had their racial bonds greatly weakened. They simply hate the thought of slavery, despise any reference to it, and turn away from anything that reminds them of it. They naturally care nothing for the songs born in slavery. They see no beauty in them, nothing commendable, nothing worth while. They do not study them, because obviously they are not fit subjects for serious thought. Among this group, Negro Folk Music finds least favor.

There are some schools attended largely by northern Negroes where the students flatly refuse to sing these songs. This is due to the fact that these students have the idea (which is often correct) that white people are looking for amusement in their singing. Some

Negroes enjoy being laughed at, but they are not found in the schools. The same students assume the attitude that the rest of the world concedes to the Negroes the ability to execute well their own music, but it is beyond them to understand and execute the classics, and any attempt to do this is presumptious. To them, this is another form of circumscription which has been a hindrance and handicap. They cannot afford to recognize any limitation, except those which confine the abilities of the whole human race. Some look upon this music with disfavor, because they simply cannot do otherwise. They have been thoroughly overwhelmed by that powerful propaganda, which aims at impressing upon the Negro his nothingness, or at best his inferiority to other races. In their desperate effort to prove they are something, they fatuously struggle to abandon that self which the world deems inferior, and to become some other self. They repudiate everything which bears the stamp of race. It is cause for sincere congratulation to ourselves that this class is growing proportionally smaller as time passes. It will finally disappear.

To those of the second generation of freedmen who live in the South, these songs are a source of encouragement. They read their story with open minds and hearts. They tell the story of our fathers' agony, the cleansing fire into which they were cast. It tells how they emerged from the fires unharmed and without the smell of smoke upon their garments, how character was brightened and faith strengthened. It tells our fathers' sublime standard of spirituality, which their children must make their very own. When they read this story and comprehend its meaning, when they catch the vision of the past, joyfully cry, "Thanks be to God for our fathers!" To be children of such forbears is a blessed inspiration; to be the heirs of such wealth of wisdom as our fathers' songs is in itself transcendant.

"Keep a-inching, Keep a-inching along,
  Jesus will come bye and bye;
Keep a-inching along like a poor inch worm,
  Jesus will come bye and bye."

"Goin' to hold out to the end,
Goin' to hold out to the end;
Let trials come as they will come,
Goin' to hold out to the end."

"Made my vow to the Lord,
And I never will turn back;
I will go, I shall go,
To see what the end will be."

"He sees all you do,
He hears all you say;
My Lord is writing all the time.
Run, Mourner, run,
Low, says the Bible;
Run, Mourner, run
Low is the way."

"Prayer is the key to Heaven,
Faith unlocks the door."

These are some of the golden thoughts of which these songs are full. They are ever calling us from discouragement and fears, they lead us to face with confidence the hostile forces of life. Because we have such fathers and such inheritance, we are ashamed not to be striving ever and ever onward and upward, we are ashamed not to do our best. It nerves us to fight. To their understanding of our fathers more than to any other cause, is due this agreeable difference between this second generation of southern Negroes and other classes. In conclusion it must be stated that though the different groups are affected in their regard for this music, by time, place, and environment and consequently make different manifestations of their regard, deep down in their hearts they share a common feeling. Though all may not sing these songs openly, they sing them in their souls. They are a part of the very breath they breathe, and of the life they live. They influence their lives and help mould their character.

SWING LOW

1. I looked over Jordan, and what did I see, Coming for to carry me home? A band of angels coming after me, Coming for to carry me home.
2. If you get there before I do, Coming for to carry me home; Tell all my friends I'm coming too, Coming for to carry me home.
3. I'm sometimes up, I'm sometimes down, Coming for to carry me home; But still my soul feels heavenly bound, Coming for to carry me home.

CHAPTER X.

A Painted Picture of a Soul.

"To seek the truth, wherever it leads,
To live the life of Love, whatever it costs;
This is to be the friend and helper of God."

IT is with a full sense of responsibility and of accountability, and, I hope, it is with due reverence that I shall now lead you, dear reader, into the presence of a soul,—this "sanctum sanctorum of life," stripped of every covering which civilization has thrown about it, the naked Ego of our race. It must seem the climax of presumption and the essence of blasphemy to make even the slightest pretense of laying open the well-springs of our life, and presenting to view the very essence of that which gives us class, name, and distinction from other men. My apology? In these days of misunderstanding, injustice, and readjustments, when the best in man is fighting for the right, when the spirit of brotherhood is waging so heroic a struggle for supremacy, whose victory means the efficaciousness of Christ's death; in the presence of these portentous facts, any thought which can shed so much as one ray of light upon the darkness of the struggle ought to be expressed.

There should not be so many unanswered questions about the Negro. Since he is so momentous a problem, he ought to be studied scientifically and the truth about him sought, found, and proclaimed. Of all the problems that face the human race, the problem of the Negro is the least scientifically studied. It is far and away the most important problem which is before our country for solution, and it is the most unwisely treated.

The black man is a great obstruction to the white man's Christianity. Except for the Negro the principle of brotherhood would doubtless be in forceful operation to-day; now it is a mountainous difficulty for the white man to accept the black man as brother, but it is an eternal verity that Christianity can never reach its ultimate saving power, it can never put forth its full flower of perfection until every man accepts every other man as his brother. Brotherhood is the business of life. With these words of explanation, let us go on to the sanctum. Our journey will lead us through a tangled waste; it will be necessary to clear away and tear up by the roots much that civilization has produced, for some of the traits which men call characteristic of Negro soul, are the plain excrescences of civilization; which, although they influence him, are not essential but accidental.

To be sure, the black man is afflicted with many of the defects and weaknesses with which other men are afflicted, and like all other branches of the human family, he is fearfully and wonderfully made; these faults are characteristic of the genus homo, and not peculiar to the Ethiopian species. The faults of humanity are well known; it is ours to seek the unknown, the soul of the American Negro. However it may seem, it is not fanciful to portray the "Painted Picture of a Soul" in colors of music. This music is his own; and the only means of expressing his life. Folk Song is the unguarded, spontaneous expression of a people's soul. It is their natural means of communication, which they understand among themselves. We know for a fact that it was never intended that the world should understand the slave music. It was a kind of secret pass-word into their lives. In some instances their secrets are protected by dual meanings to their songs. "Steal Away to Jesus" meant to the slave a secret meeting which the master had prohibited; and to the overseer and the rest of the world, a longing for the quiet communion with God. "Rise! Shine! For the Light is a-Coming!" meant to the slave, freedom approaching! To the world it was the Messianic prophecy. "Keep a-Inching Along, Jesus Will Come Bye and Bye," means to the slave that freedom would come in answer to faithful prayer and service; to the world, conversion. "Great Camp Meeting in the Promised Land" and "Good News, the Chariot's a-Coming, Don't Yer Leave Me Behind" were to the slaves prophecies of the joys of freedom; to the uninitiated, anticipations of joy in Heaven.

Man generally tells the truth in secret. "As a man thinketh in his heart, so is he," and he will generally express what he thinks if he is not to be charged with it afterwards. This was just the attitude, condition, and environment of the Negro slave. So the only source of authentic information, the only reliable source of truth in regard to the fundamentals of his character, is his songs. In making this investigation extending over a decade, all available publications were consulted, all possible byways and highways were searched, as many ex-slaves as possible were conferred with, and every available person who knew anything was questioned. From these sources there have been gathered about five hundred songs and fragments of songs. These have all been analyzed and their thoughts and sentiments gathered. These are the colors in which the soul is painted.

The first is the rich color of Home Love, as expressed in the home songs. It is a striking fact that the best known and the most dearly beloved of Stephen Foster's songs are his best imitations of the Negro Folk Songs, and they sing the love of home. "The Old Folks at Home" and "Kentucky Home" are generally classed as Negro music. In his very life, the black man portrays himself a home-loving being. He is no willing wanderer, and whatever spot he adopts as his home has his full devotion. "Way Down Upon the Sewanee River" paints for him a vision of love and happiness. So strong are these home ties that Heaven, Canaan, the Promised Land, and the Kingdom, mean nothing more nor less than home. As glorious as he knows Heaven to be with all its joys, peace, rest, crowns, harps, robes, angels, and God, home comprehends it all.

The next is the powerful color of prayer. It is one of the emphatic forces of his soul.

"Ask and it shall be given,
Seek and you shall find,
Knock and the door shall be opened."

"Prayer is the key of Heaven."

If there is any life to which prayer means more than to that of the Negro, in what part of God's universe can it be found? Who has tested the power of prayer more severely than he? Who has proved more than he its efficacy? Not only in his closet and on his knees has he lifted up his heart in petition, but he has sped his pleadings on the pinions of song.

"O Lord, O my Lord—
O my Good Lord—
Keep me from sinking down."

"Lord, I want to be like Jesus
In-a my heart."

This Jesus, like whom he prayed to be, was the One he knew to have been the Great Servant, the One who said He came not to be ministered unto, but to minister, and this spirit of service is one of the regnant forces of his own life. This life of service from one viewpoint was apparently wrought out by a superior power well-nigh irresistible, the system of slavery, but away down under the overwhelming and crushing force was that humble sacrificing spirit, which though misguided, misdirected and over-awed, still had the essence of Christlikeness.

Humility was taught him by every power of nature. He learned from the heavens, the mountains, the storms, and the will of masters, that his duty was to be humble. He sang humility in—

"Live a humble."

"Lord, make me more humble."

"Lord, I want to be more."

"Takes a humble soul to join us,
In the army of the Lord."

"Low is the way—"

"Heaven is so high, and I am so low,
I don't know if I'll ever get to Heaven or no."

It is a great wonder that the Negro, during the period which witnessed the birth of these heart songs, should make any expression of love for the world. It is, of course, explainable that he should love his own kind, those of his own blood, who were suffering with him, but that he should express love for God who permitted his sufferings, and for the man who inflicted them, is wonderful! But he did in forty of his songs, express love for God and the world, which means that by love he was possessed and mightily ruled. Otherwise, the blight of desolation would have hovered where the smile of prosperity beamed upon our land. For love is stronger than hate, and is ever engaged in the sanctification of the heart wherein it abides. It were valueless to wage any discussion as to the causes that produce this phenomenon of a suffering slave, manacled and shackled, singing and living a brotherly love, the all important fact is that this phenomenon was a real, live force in the heart of these, God's children.

One of the noblest fruits of love is patience. Because God's black child loved his Father, he was willing to accept as wise his Father's dispensation, and walk, almost without complaint or question the dark, stormy, thorny path he could not see, and endure meekly the sorrow-laden life which he could not understand. Because he loved his fellows, he was willing to bear with their shortcomings, feeling that if he should "wait a little while," man's humanity would assert itself, and bring to him opportunity and happiness, all the more extensive and deep because he endured so long and so painfully. In the awful struggle between inhumanity and patience, patience triumphed, and patience triumphant is what the slave has wrought out and presented to the world, and still he cries, "Lord, make me more patient."

It is the common way of the world to class love, patience, and meekness among the fragile pulchritudes of human character, and to stamp as weak and pusillanimous those persons whom these qualities dominate. It is the world's way of thinking that character, to be admirable, must be a live kinetic energy, moving things before it or drawing them in the wake. Many powerful personalities, without any dirigent love for their fellows to make them benefactors, have called forth clamorous praises from the world, because they could "make things go" or could "do things." And much of the world has refused to accept as its standard the one perfect character because he did not overcome his enemies and build up his kingdom by force. But as the years come on, bringing the exigencies and crises in human affairs that try men's souls, the world is most assuredly recognizing the efficacy and beneficence of force ruled by love, patience, and meekness.

Patience breathes through all the Negro's songs, yet though he has loved, has been patient and meek almost to such a degree that the world has sometimes thought him cowardly, there is abundant proof both in his music and in his life, that the blood of a coward flows not in his veins. The most striking of his martial songs are:

"March on, and you shall gain the victory—
March on, and you shall gain the day."

"We want no cowards in our band,
We call for valiant hearted men—"

"O brethren, rise, shine, give God the glory,
For the year of Jubilee."

"Do you want to be a soldier,
For the year of Jubilee?"

"Rise, shine, for thy light is a-coming."

"I intend to fight and never stop,
Until I reach the mountain top."

"O, what do you say, brother?
O, what do you say, brother,
O, what do you say, brother,
About this Gospel War?"

"I will die in the field,
Stay in the field,
Stay in the field, brother,
Stay in the field,
Until the War is ended."

"Fight," "battle," and "war" are important words in his vocabulary, and his record for courage shames him not. The slaves who faced perennial dangers while protecting inviolate the women, children, and homes of their absent masters; the multitudes of freedmen who met and overcame unspeakable opposition during those dark, uncertain days following the Emancipation Proclamation; Crispus Attucks, in Boston, Massachusetts; Peter Salem, at Bunker Hill; the men who stood with Jackson at New Orleans; the Fifty-fourth Massachusetts which smiled at death before Fort Wagner; those black regiments who have hallowed the West, the Philippines, and the West Indies with their blood; and the millions in civil life who are forever contending in mortal combat with the hydra and the fiery dragon, attest the Negro's courage.

Great souls are souls of great faith. Great faith is a mighty weapon for fighting battles and winning victories. No faithless, doubting soul has been a positive blessing to mankind, but that soul with an abiding, immutable belief in "omnipotent righteousness" has ever been the "salt of the earth," and it is a deep satisfaction to the Negro himself that he is no doubter but a positive believer; that his own soul finds no overmatching difficulty in holding to his faith in his God, but that he willingly trusts to omniscence, fully expecting the final triumph of justice. Judged by his own soul-thoughts, if there can be any comparison of virtues, his supreme virtue is his faith; for every one of his songs is a song of faith. It is true that there are some individual songs which have faith for a theme, such as—

"All I want is a little more faith in Jesus";

"Faith unlocks the door," and

"Lord, make me more faithful,"

but from the nature of the case, these must be few, for faith is the all-pervading power of all the Negro's music.

A most natural consequence of having faith is having joy, for the soul that believes that all things will eventuate according to the laws of right, and that "God's in his Heaven," has joy in his security. Truly, clouds sometimes overcast the skies, but these are only incidents in the life of faith. The believer can smile through tears and shout Hallelujah! in a minor strain. So, for every sorrow song like "Nobody Knows the Trouble I See," there are many of those blasts of joy, like "Great Camp Meeting," "Shout All Over God's Heaven," and "Golden Slippers." The Negro has the habit of being happy.

His endurance is a child of his faith and his hope. What a child it is! What power! What prodigious strength! What an Atlas, bearing what a world! The Maker made the African strong that he might endure. What has he endured? What no other would,— cruel wrath, and the folly of man, the hidden face of God, Gethsemane, and Calvary,—that here on this western continent opportunity might be given for the growth of a nation which should be a mighty instrument in the strong right hand of God. The songs of endurance are pointed and positive:

"Goin' to hold out to the end,
Let trials come as they will come—"

"Keepa--inching along; Jesus will come by and by."

"Made my vow to the Lord;
Never will turn back;
I will go, shall go,
To see what the end will be."

"Stand the storm, it won't be long,
We'll anchor by and by."

His soul is strengthened with hope, else why would he strive, endure, and be patient? How could he? If he had not been sure that a better day was coming, all that remained for him would have been renunciation of all strivings and aspirations, giving himself up to the things of this world, exacting an eye for an eye and a tooth for a tooth. He sang his hope in such songs as—

"Goin' to see my Jesus,

"Goin' to see my Jesus,
Some of these mornings
Hope I'll join the band."

"I hope to meet my brother there,
Who used to join with me in prayer."

Thus we find faith, hope, patience, endurance, prayer, joy, courage, and humility and the love of mankind, of home, and of God to be the salient qualities of the Negro's soul. Such is the testimony of the only true expression of his soul, his songs. Yet were there no songs to record these, they could be seen reflected in his life. With these virtues, his regnant forces, it is not difficult to account for his progress. On the other hand, it is quite difficult to understand why he receives such unbrotherly treatment at the hands of his brothers. If not to others, it is certainly a wonder to the later generation of Negroes, that in spite of such unwholesome and positively pernicious conditions as the system of slavery generated, our forbears possessed and developed such souls, and although the story brings tears to our eyes, our hearts swell with pride that we can claim such ancestors many of whom are still with us (blessed be their beloved heads!) with their sweet inspirations.

From the extent to which the different qualities of the Negro soul are emphasized it is clear that his fundamentals are strong, pure, and abundant. Also it would seem that he believes more in the efficiency of the propulsive power of hope, than in the impulsive power of fear, more in love than in fear. The greatest emphasis was laid upon virtue and, as Seneca says:

"Virtue, alone, raises us above fears."

The picture is before you: Virtues powerfully blended upon an ample background of love, energized by the spirit of the eternal. It is not a picture of perfection, for there are daubings here and there which civilization has smeared, but these are overshadowed by the sublimity of the artist's conception. This picture, although most beautiful to us, their children, cannot express all there is of our fathers' souls, for, as Bacon says:

"The best part of beauty is that which no picture can express."

A PAINTED PICTURE OF A SOUL.

LORD, I WANT TO BE A CHRISTIAN

1. Lord, I want to be a Chris-tian In a my heart, in a my heart, Lord, I want to be a Chris-tian In a my heart.
2. Lord, I want to be more lov-ing In a my heart, in a my heart, Lord, I want to be more lov-ing In a my heart.
3. Lord, I want to be more ho-ly In a my heart, in a my heart, Lord, I want to be more ho-ly In a my heart.
4. I don't want to be like Ju-das In a my heart, in a my heart, I don't want to be like Ju-das In a my heart.
5. Lord, I want to be like Je-sus In a my heart, in a my heart, Lord, I want to be like Je-sus In a my heart.

REFRAIN.

In a my heart,............ In a my heart,............
In a my heart, In a my heart,
Lord, I want to be a Chris-tian In a my heart.

The Jubilee Songs and Fisk University

are companion facts. Fisk is the special home of the Jubilee music and gave that music its name. The Jubilee Singers saved Fisk University, as has been shown in this book. Fisk has always paid a great deal of attention to music, and the graduates of the School of Music are sought for by many more schools than can be supplied. A music building is a crying need. Fisk would also take upon herself new and larger tasks is the discovery and development of the folk songs of the South and in their forms of service among the musical people of the South. Dreams of great service wait on sufficient resources.
¶ Fisk University includes a standard college for Negro education, with four-year courses in Arts, Science, Home Economics and Education. It is expected to make these four college courses ever increasingly stronger and better. This will involve larger expenditures, but it is believed that friends of education will help, as they realize what Fisk and and Fisk graduates are doing for the race and the nation. Aid is solicited in sums of any amount, from very small to very large. Whatever aids a student to live at Fisk or aids Fisk to train leaders of high power and keen good will, will strengthen the nation and hasten the era of peace of earth.
¶ Fisk aims to train leaders in education, in the church, in the professions, and in business. The magnitude of the work which Fisk shall do will depend upon the resources placed at her disposal.